Fanthology

Edited by
Robert Endeacott & Graeme Garvey

Relish Books

First published in 2004 by Relish Books,
Leeds, West Yorkshire, UK

www.relishbooks.co.uk

ISBN 0-9547844-1-3

Cover Design: Chris Archer. Billy Bremner original image used with kind
permission of © ColorSport
Other photographs courtesy of the Yorkshire Evening Post (Yorkshire Post
Newspapers)

General Design Editor: Andy Searle, The Parrs Wood Press

Printed by Gráficas Rigel. Spain
www.graficasrigel.com

Distributed by Gardners Books, Eastbourne

A Catalogue for this book is available from the British Library.

Dedicated to my kids (who are Leeds fans)
and all you Leeds fans out there
- *Graeme Garvey.*

To Bethany & Matthew, to my Family &
Friends and to everyone who enjoys
Fanthology - *Robert Endeacott.*

Fanthology Contents

Foreword

I was immensely proud to be asked to contribute to this fine book. I was born and bred in Leeds, but Leeds' magnificent support is not confined to Yorkshire, or indeed this country. Throughout my near 40 year 'career' as a Leeds United fan I have met the cream of the land in terms of Fanaticism. This book will take you through the highs and lows of some of these followers. I know several top supporters from other football clubs, but I can say without the slightest hesitation that no club comes close to the number of loyal fans as this great club of ours. Fans who think nothing of travelling across to the other side of the world, literally at the drop of a hat, for a mere friendly. I was among a bunch of such supporters who travelled to Japan, on a ramshackle old Russian aeroplane, for a friendly game in Tokyo. We arrived for the game on a Monday evening in 1991, returning the following day to be in Leeds in time to attend a minor West Riding County Cup game against Halifax Town on the Wednesday.

Thanks mainly due to Don Revie and to some extent John Charles, Leeds United Football Club is known throughout the world. The LUFC flag is flown proudly from Key West in Florida to the far corners of Australia, throughout Ireland, Europe and Scandinavia.

In 1973 Leeds played AC Milan in the European Cup Winners' Cup Final in Thessaloniki in Greece. The referee, who incidentally was Greek, chose to favour the Italians that evening and following a 1-0 victory, he was banned for life amidst allegations of bribery and corruption. The Greeks have never forgotten or forgiven Christos Michas and to this day have a strong affection for Leeds United. This was evident only recently. Despite being relegated from the Premiership, Leeds were invited to open the newly revamped Kaftanzoglio football stadium in Thessaloniki. They were of course, accompanied as ever by devoted Leeds fans representing the north, south, east and west of Britain.

FANTHOLOGY

A few years ago, Leeds played the Israeli side Hapoel Tel Aviv in Florence in Italy. There, in a bar near the ground, I met Nano, a fanatical Italian Leeds fan, sporting long black hair, wearing denims and draped in a Union Jack with Leeds United emblazoned across it. Whilst working in London in the late 80's and early 90's, Nano had seen Leeds on television and fell in love with them. Lots of continental Leeds fans prefer to travel alone to watch The Whites. Geir from Norway has been a regular to these shores ever since the mid-70's. Hilary from Malta has supported Leeds ever since they rolled into Valletta back in 1979. Another loyal traveller is Ziggi, who hails from Lierse in Belgium (where incidentally there is a bar called 'Elland Road' that has a large cardboard cut-out of David Batty as well as other Leeds memorabilia adorning the walls.) Ex-pat Perry makes regular visits back to his hometown Leeds from thousands of miles away in Key West. He actually flew to every Champions' League game in Europe back in 2001/02. Craig Gill from Adelaide is amongst many thousands of Australian-based Leeds fans. And don't get me started on the Irish (the North and Republic), particularly the Belfast lot, their regular pilgrimages to the city centre of Leeds are legendary.

Robert Endeacott and Graeme Garvey, with Fanthology will introduce you to Leeds fans from all walks of life, as well as players, each with their own memories of Leeds United Football Club. You don't necessarily have to be a Leeds fan to enjoy this book, as most fans will relate to the turbulent thrills (and chills) threaded throughout its pages. If you're not a Leeds fan however, please feel free to climb aboard and join the 'Elite'.

Enjoy!

Gary Edwards.

Introduction

Good morning Leeds United fans. Or *good afternoon* or even *good evening* depending on where you are and which continent you're presently residing in. That's something to remember: there are relatives of the Leeds United Supporters' Family in differing time zones and in nearly every country in the world, certainly in every continent (bar Antarctica perhaps and even then I wouldn't bet on it). There's something very comforting knowing we Leeds fans are in existence all over the globe and it's reassuring to know that while you're reading this, other Leeds fans on faraway edges of the planet will be reading it at er, the same *moment*.

When times are hard, not only in football but in life, to know someone else is feeling the same frustrations, dilemmas or aches of the heart really does matter. There's genuine comfort in the knowledge of there always being at least one fellow supporter experiencing the same feelings. Isn't 'support' another word for comfort after all? There is certainly at least an element of truth in the saying 'A problem shared is a problem halved' and let's face it, we Leeds supporters know more than most about problems.

With Fanthology - via Fanthology might be a better way of putting it - we wanted to hear from Leeds fans 'why' they are Leeds fans, to give them a blank canvas/page to tell the world. What is it about Leeds United that these unquestioning, unwavering followers love, what is it that makes them tick; what is it that makes them sick? Okay, we didn't really want to hear about the sick part, we've all had too much unappetising fare to stomach already, especially in recent years. There's a great gallows-humour spirit within the Leeds following but Fanthology isn't the place for it, it's a positive celebration and commemoration of what it means and feels and matters to be a Leeds fan, to BE Leeds. We may not have won every trophy going (and I know we'll never win the FA Cup again!) but that doesn't dilute the fact that Leeds United Football Club is the greatest football club on earth and the best team in the land to support.

When I was a sprog, we were that poor…
We weren't the richest of families in South Leeds, that's for sure. Not that it's important anyway, because I still became a very privileged kid from around 1971 when my Dad Barry got a job on the ground staff at Elland Road. So many stories and rumours I could tell - some I'd better not for legal reasons - and I know there are hundreds, thousands of Leeds fans with just as many if not more (and better) tales to recount. My mate Cruncher for one thing - I'll get the info out of you one day, Chris, and your dad!

We did invite many more contributors and there were alas, many we were unable to reach. But don't worry, we're very hopeful Fanthology will be the first in a series, as long as people buy it then we'll publish it! So, look to the end of this book to find out how to get in touch - contributions to Fanthology 2 are already invited - so please, get thinking, get writing.

Leeds players, for most of the time, are our heroes in white, yellow and blue, and they form the skeleton of this great club. The fans represent the flesh and lifeforce of the club. Combined, *united*, the players and fans provide the heart, the tissue and of course the vital organs - without each other, there'd be no point in Leeds United or any football club actually existing.

Events, occasions and incidents related to Leeds United hold different sensations and levels of significance for each of us. What might seem trivial to some, matters greatly to others. Fanthology contains trivia and nonsense sitting (well, standing most of the

INTRODUCTION

time) comfortably on the terraces next to deeply meaningful and spiritual moments. All depending on your perspective obviously and whether your view is impeded by a pillar or a seven foot tall/wide fan in front.

Personally, I could go on (*and on and on*) with little stories over the years relating to Leeds United. Would anyone be really interested though? Did Geoff Hurst's shot really cross the line in 1966? Were most 70's European referees crooked? Here's a few memory morsels...

Am I the only one who even now gets a tad emotional recalling Vinnie Jones spending time before matches chatting to disabled and wheelchair-using Leeds fans in the West Stand? I sincerely doubt it.

And it might not matter much in the whole scheme of things but to me, one morning as a five year old, standing with my Dad, squinting up at the enormous god like presence of World Cup winning hero Jackie Charlton, meant a great deal. He was never my favourite player but everything he's ever done in life - including his autobiography - holds great credence for me, beginning with that encounter. We were nearby his scarf and souvenir stall and I've no idea what was said or if my Dad bought me anything (I wager he didn't) but it was an Event with a capital 'e' for me. And to this day I can't quite get over the fact that Our Jack was talking to us on a Saturday morning, just a few hours before a game in which he'd be wearing the legendary blue number 5 on the legendary white Leeds shirt again.

And the time with my two Ian mates, Lem and Acky, stopping off at a little corner shop (now part of a picturesque car park) on Elland Road en route to Matthew Murray High School, was a lovely moment. We met Maurice Lindley and, in hushed excitement we'd exclaimed 'It's Maurice Lindley!' Hearing us, it was clear we'd made his day, he was without doubt delighted. To think that a real gentleman of the game and a star of Don Revie's backroom team was thrilled to be shaking our hands still makes me proud. He didn't buy us any sweets though.

The time when my Dad got me in to the players' tunnel before a game. So many Leeds officials were so friendly to me and so interesting to just watch. Bob English (another behind-the-play star) kindly threw me an orange. I dropped it. Embarrassing but not a crucial turning point of my childhood as I never looked to be the next David Harvey, I was always going to be the next hot shot bar-breaking Peter Lorimer. And I couldn't forget a steamy glimpse of Paul Madeley after one game, sitting on a changing room bench absolutely exhausted and absolutely in the nude, and I'll never be able to completely erase from my senses the stench Gordon McQueen left in the Gents' before one game. He must have been very nervous, that's all I need to say. I made sure I avoided both rooms ever since.

And by heck I miss the floodlights. Why oh why oh why did it happen, how was it allowed to happen? They were beautiful, they were monumental, they were British landmarks and they were blooming great, bigger and brighter than a Lucas Radebe smile. Were there ever any higher floodlights in the whole world? Did the governors of Leeds city have no soul? To quote (Jackie) Charlton Heston in Planet of the Apes: 'Damn you, you fools!' (or something like that).

The times are numerous when my actual life - as a boy or man - felt boosted by simple straightforward acknowledgements, greetings and even just ordinary smiles from, in my mind,

INTRODUCTION

extraordinary people. Men like Eddie Gray, Duncan McKenzie, Gary Kelly, and David Batty have put a spring in to my step a few times (not necessarily a good thing in the case of Kels and Batts as I was legless on both occasions). But why should it all matter so much, they are only men after all, it is only a football club?

Well it's obvious isn't it? Or it will be, once you've read the following 200 or so pages!

Robert Endeacott, 2004

Chapter 1

Choosing/Being Chosen By Leeds

For many fans, following the club is a lifelong journey. How it all began though, is not the same for everyone. Many were brought up in a Leeds United household but for others it was much less straightforward. What seems clear is that, once it's in the blood, you'll never support anyone else.

<u>Pure and simple</u>

Neil Jeffries - I don't have to speak to anyone about my love and memories of Leeds United for very long before they ask me, 'So how come you support Leeds?' It's the accent. Gets 'em every time. I've done my best to iron out the worst traces of my native Suffolk tongue and I've lived in London since 1982 - but there's no way I'll ever pass for a Yorkshireman. So I smile, take a deep breath, and admit how old I am.

When I was a boy of eight going on nine, Leeds were a fast rising team who played their home games 200 miles away from Lowestoft, the town I was born in. Neither of my parents were football fans and so I guess I became one as a result of peer pressure. Actually, I don't think there was much pressure, it was the most natural thing in the world for a young boy in 1968/69 to kick a ball around the streets and to covet a football shirt.

Every weekend we'd get on our bikes and ride to Normaston Park, one of us with a shiny orange, plastic football hanging in a string-bag from the handlebars, all of us in our favourite team's shirts.

Matching shorts and socks, too, if we were lucky. The park was 27 miles from Norwich but canary yellow shirts were nowhere to be seen. Lowestoft's own non-league side and the county's top side of Ipswich Town played in blue but the only lads wearing that colour were fans of Everton - for they were a top six side in those days. But mostly, my schoolmates were running around in the red of Manchester United.

You think glory hunters are a modern phenomenon? A product of Sky TV and the digital age? Think again. Man U were as popular in the provinces then as they are now. They'd won the league in 1967 and in the Roman Hill area of Lowestoft were the team of choice. But not for me. Although as mesmerised as anyone by the skills of George Best, my infant heart had been won by something far purer. As pure as the driven snow, actually. Snow with a hint of owl. The white shirts of Leeds United.

Why white? Hell, I don't really know. Maybe some deep-rooted association that a psychiatrist could unravel but I do remember that white to me was just the ultimate. Sure, it got dirty the quickest, but when you could have any colour or combination of colours you wanted and Subbuteo team catalogues to help you choose, it was something really special to opt for no colour at all, to opt for white. Thinking about it now, white implied total confidence and an implicit belief that simple efficiency was best. Stripes and contrasting sleeves were a sign of insecurity. Bright colours a distraction, some kind of camouflage to hide certain weakness.

And so the team for me was Leeds United. It was my shirt, rather than my skills, which made me stand out on Normaston Park and I was proud to wear it. I was never hugely comfortable with the owl badge that my mum sewed onto it for me. I'd bought the badge, printed on a small square of material which I still own today, from

CHOOSING/BEING CHOSEN BY LEEDS

Sam Hooks in Bevan Street for pennies. It wasn't so much the stitchwork I didn't like, although the hem made me feel like I had a beer mat on my chest, more the fact that it spoiled the purity of the white shirt. Suddenly it was partly blue. Even today I shudder at all the trimmings and logos that adorn modern kits. But back in 1969 I was about to get the ultimate reward, the team I had chosen would overtake Man U and Everton and all the rest and finish top of the league. White had triumphed and Leeds were champions. It was as pure and simple and true as that. I never looked back.

Neil Jeffries

The Crunch

Why and when as a schoolgirl living in Kent did I begin to support Leeds United? Well, originally and to my shame now, my first team was Man United, but let me explain as there was a very good reason for choosing that club at the time. I lived in a small village called Yalding in the heart of the Kent countryside. Also living in the village and going to school with my two much older brothers was a boy called David Sadler who was developing into a talented footballer. This boy became a local hero when he was later signed to play for that Lancashire team, alongside the likes of George Best and Bobby Charlton. Almost everyone in the village instantly became fans of the club the local lad now played for, including my brothers and me.

As I got older, around the age of twelve I became more interested in football and started to watch more matches on tv. I became captivated by the Leeds United team who were great to watch, I really liked the way they played. There were other reasons that attracted me to them. I liked the fact that they played all in white, which was different. I liked the owl emblem on the shirts, I had

17

always liked owls. Also, I had boys in my class at school with the surnames Clarke, Giles and Jones and this amused me at the time. I also began to feel sorry for the team when after playing so well, they would lose an important cup game or come second in the league. They began to find a place in my heart.

The crunch came in 1970 when Man U including David Sadler played Leeds in a series of replay matches in the semi final of the FA Cup, the dilemma was who to support. When it came to the second replay which was televised, my heart ruled and I chose Leeds who eventually won the game and went on to face Chelsea in the Final. On that Cup Final day I had truly become a fully-fledged Leeds supporter and remain so to this day. The highs and lows, the anguish and despair of that game which we fully deserved to win, and then the drama of the replay cemented my allegiance to the team.

Well, that was the start and when the new season began, I got together with a friend and we travelled to watch Leeds each time they played a game in London. I now feel very privileged to have been able to watch the team in the Revie years. We only managed one trip to Elland Road in those days as we were still at school and not earning, but it was a memorable trip. My favourite player of the time was Terry Cooper as I loved the way he played, overlapping on the wing and then supplying that vital ball to our strikers.

I now live in Winchester in Hampshire and still love the team I chose all those years ago. Two of my sons carry on the tradition and also support Leeds. It's been a tough few years recently for us loyal supporters, but I am looking forward with renewed optimism.

Marching on together and forever,

Lynn Murnaghan.

Why Leeds? - Little Billy Bremner

Born in Colchester, Essex on 21st August 1955, I took no interest at all in football in my early years. My father was a season ticket holder at Ipswich Town and went with a friend to every match, but for one game, during the 1968/69 season, his friend couldn't attend so my father asked me if I would like to go. Well it seemed a better choice than doing my homework so I went travelling the nineteen miles from Colchester.

Being only thirteen, I stood at the front edge of the terrace and looked at the players live and close up for the first time. To see the size of Jack Charlton next to Billy Bremner was awesome. I don't remember much about the game only that wee Billy stood out to me as such a leader who commanded those around him and, although small in stature, did not shirk any of the tackles. As Billy stood out so much to me, I wanted to see him again even more than with the rest of the team.

I pleaded with my father to let me go to another match. This time it was against Arsenal at Highbury and Leeds won 2-1. After this I could not get enough of Leeds and continued to see as many matches as possible. I did meet Billy, once, after Leeds had beaten Ipswich during the 1973/74 season. We travelled on the same train back towards London and I managed to get him to autograph my rosette.

I believe that any supporter who has been with the team from the late sixties up to this season has had far more highs and lows than with any other football team. This however has not deterred me from following them and no one can take away my memories of the man who was Leeds United.

Tom Smith

Paul's Choice

Why Leeds? Because it had to be different to Burnley or Bradford City or Bradford Park Avenue. These were the teams the other boys at my school supported. For some reason I didn't want to go along with the crowd. I lived in a small village near Bradford, just over the hill from the Yorkshire, Lancashire border. The time had arrived when the playing of football had to be complemented by allegiance to a particular side so that you could pretend to be your favourite player.

At my school, the rule was that if you supported a First Division side it was Burnley, who, as this was the early sixties, were still a team to be reckoned with. If you wanted to go 'local', then it was Bradford City or Park Avenue. Neither of these teams had set pulses racing for many years. At best they brought a sort of excitement to their respective supporters by playing a kind of football hokey cokey through promotion from and relegation to the Fourth Division. If they really felt devilish they would, on occasion, court real danger by applying to the then Football League old boys club' for re-election.

Despite these not too encouraging performances, I'd toyed with throwing my allegiance behind Bradford City. But then, after I had carefully counted the number of Avenue supporters amongst the older boys in the school, I had thought better of it. The younger boys spent the week before local derbies trying to avoid their physical inquisitions as to whether you were 'City' or 'Avenue'.

There was then the problem of being chased by the rump of City supporters, who through their tear flooded eyes, were noting which renegades were switching allegiance in the cause of self

20

preservation, so that they could exact payment for bruises suffered supporting their team. Supporting Burnley didn't help their very few followers, as they just got thumped by everyone.

I remembered that the previous year there had been a boy in my class who had said he supported a team from Scotland called the Hibs. This had perplexed the Park Avenue hit squad, who didn't seem to know how to deal with a name which was not one of the usual suspects and my Scots pal was left alone, more by pity rather than through fear or hatred. This seemed a possible solution to a sticky situation. The problem was they would only make a single exception so it wouldn't work for me and, anyway, I wanted to support a successful team.

This was going to be a choice that I would have to live with for the rest of my life, because that is what you did in those days, you stuck with one team forever, so it should be a team with which I could share more highs than lows. Little did I know how often these questionable sentiments would come back to haunt me over the next forty years or so.

Such an important decision needed a second opinion and, besides, I had exhausted my knowledge of football teams. I had heard of a team called Northern, but wasn't too sure whether they were a football team and I didn't want to show my ignorance by asking someone at school. I needed some older counsel. I would ask my best friend, who was also called Paul, which was handy if you wanted to stay out longer when your mum was calling you in. You could always say that you thought it was the other Paul's mum who was calling him. Paul had the benefit of an extra eighteen months' life experience and an uncle who played for the local cricket team and who provided Paul with lots of up to date information about sport in general.

After listening carefully to my predicament, Paul remained quiet for a few moments as if trying to take in the true gravity of the situation. Then, in a calm, deliberate voice he said it. He said the name that I, over the next forty-odd years, would come to cheer on, to curse over, to berate, to cry out at, to shout at, to scream at, to roar at, to praise, to criticise, to laugh at even and to despair of. But never to forsake.

I would pass it on to my sons, albeit after a brief dalliance by them with Keegan's Newcastle, which I put down to a momentary lack of attention on my part in not putting them right after a particularly over-complimentary commentator on Sky. But all of this was before an unknown future obviously. I listened as my friend repeated the name in case I hadn't quite taken it in, 'Leeds.'

I thought for a moment and then said, 'Why?' I could have asked 'where?' my geographic knowledge failing me. Paul explained to me that his Uncle Frank had been telling him that Leeds United had been unlucky not to win the First Division the previous season, had got through to the FA Cup Final and that they were going to be, what his uncle had called 'a force to be reckoned with' over the next few years. In fact, they played in an all white kit like Real Madrid, so they must be good. What was more, Paul said that Leeds wasn't very far from Bradford so I might be able to get my dad to take us both to see them play.

It all seemed to fall into place. A team no one else at school supported, who were successful and not too far away, but far enough to avoid triggering any painful local rivalries at school. My mind was made up, this was to be my team. Then a thought struck me. If you supported a team you had to have a scarf in their colours. But Leeds played in all white didn't they? Even for a nine-year-old boy of the sixties, for whom the height of fashion was tucking his shirt in, an all white scarf just didn't seem right. What would my mates think? Still worse what would they say? It was no good, I decided that I would have to think of an alternative team to support.

Some friends at school had some football cards from packets of tea and after a close inspection of a few dog-eared examples I decided that the blue of Chelsea was a colour I could cope with and, more importantly, one which I felt would be less open to peer ridicule. Still, there was a small tinge of disappointment in being unable to go with my first choice.

I had become quite comfortable with the name 'Leeds'. Had I had an understanding of grammar I would have probably said that it was the single syllable of their name that attracted me. It seemed to give it a forthrightness and a determination not to be messed about with. It was as if the United bit wasn't needed. There were other 'uniteds' but only one Leeds.

Agreement was made with my mum to buy me a Chelsea scarf for my birthday. Looking back many years later I smile at my naivety of expecting in the early sixties to buy a Chelsea scarf in a sports shop in Bradford. The lack of choice in these pre-replica kit days was brought home to me when the lady shop assistant asked, 'Who are they then? Are they a foreign team? Never heard of them.'

My mum asked what football scarves did they have, unaware of the careful deliberations that had gone into my original choice and thinking that one scarf was very much like another. I began to explain to her that it didn't work like that, when the assistant interrupted saying that they had Bradford City and another Bradford team's.

FANTHOLOGY

I began to be resigned to my fate, when almost as an after thought the assistant said, '...and this one that says "Leeds United' on the packet. Is that any good?'

I caught my breath and nearly spaced out as I saw blue and gold stripes spaced out across the scarf. "Is that a Leeds scarf?' I checked, not caring whether it was stupid question or not and hoping that the assistant hadn't read the wrong label.

'That's what it says, and there's a woolly hat as well with the same stripes on it,' she said laying them out on the counter. Shortly after I was walking out of the shop with my neck and head warmed by blue and gold stripes. Now I could get on with being a real supporter of what was the best team in the country.

I soon knew by heart the names of all the Leeds players and used to wait impatiently for my father to finish reading the evening newspaper so that I could scan the back page for any snippet of news about my beloved Leeds. Over time I have never been able to explain to my family the grip that the fortunes of a football team had over me. How my mood for the forthcoming week could be determined by their result at the weekend and how I continued to support them even when they caused me so much disappointment by nearly winning so much more. My passion even hid the irony when they were beaten by a now hated Chelsea in a FA Cup Final reply as if the scarf incident was hidden away, a repressed memory.

As I have said to my sons, you stick with one team forever, that's what you do.

Paul Birch

CHOOSING/BEING CHOSEN BY LEEDS

Best Leeds Team whose Surnames Start with 'C'

Carson, Cherry, Charles, Charlton, Cooper, Currie, Cantona (sorry!), Collins, Clarke, Chapman, Connor

Subs: Cush, Copping, Curtis, Cochrane

GG

The Promotion Dance

The passion I feel for my beloved Leeds United probably goes back in my own history book to 1961 when Don Revie, while still a player, was appointed the new manager. He, too, felt passionate about the team and, combining this eagerness and excitement with determination and the desire for success, achieved his goal. There were hard times but we got there.

My proudest and most memorable time was when Leeds won the 1963/64 Division Two title and we finished with, I believe, a remarkable 63 points. Reaching the First Division was celebrated by a 'Promotion Dance' held at the Astoria Ballroom on Roundhay Road, North Leeds. Like a miracle, friends of ours managed to get my boyfriend and me two tickets to attend and I just couldn't believe our luck. To be in the same company as this 'glorious eleven', Bremner, Giles, Hunter, to name but a few, was an unbelievable dream for me and still is to this day.

They were ordinary lads at heart and no one would have known any difference between them and us. They mingled with and chatted to everyone. I managed to find a scrap of paper in my handbag and achieved my ambition that wonderful evening, to have all of their autographs. That was, and always will be, my special moment.

FANTHOLOGY

Our first season in Division One saw us finish runners-up to Manchester United, pipped only on goal average. It was amazing, playing against the likes of Law and Charlton, and we achieved all this in our very first one.

Val Garrett

You can't help who you fall in love with

So how does a young boy from West London end up supporting Leeds United, and with such passion? The fact that I didn't find myself supporting a London club is quite amazing considering the amount of local bias that exists and how youngsters can be so easily influenced.

My interest in football started in 1974 when I was eight years old. My Grandad Ted started coming round for Sunday dinner and afterwards would religiously take a chair in the living room, have a smoke, and watch 'The Big Match', which had highlights of the previous day's games. That was in the era when league matches all kicked off at 3.00 on a Saturday and none were shown live.

I had only really come across a few teams at this point. My grandad supported Fulham although I never got to know this until they reached the 1975 Cup Final as he never spoke of them before then. 'The Big Match', being a London Weekend Television programme, always showed London teams and I remember West Ham frequently being featured. I particularly recall Mervyn Day and his high goal kicks, and Billy Bonds in midfield.

I never took any notice of the result of any of the games and it didn't matter to me who won or lost. It was just football on the television and no more than that. Clearly, though, West Ham didn't do it for me. I did however seem to try and latch myself onto a team, although in a less conventional fashion. My sister used to wear her Bay City Rollers' scarf around her wrist. Taking a leaf out of her book, I decided to do the same with my Mum's yellow and green check scarf and for a while would wear that round my wrist at home or while out shopping with my Mum, and in my head pretend to myself it was a Norwich City scarf. This didn't last for long though as I guess the novelty wore off, with the scarf, and thus with Norwich City.

In my last year at junior school I came so close to being a Leeds supporter but it was a path at the time I chose not to take. Two teachers started taking about ten of us out one afternoon each week to play football. One wore a Chelsea kit and the other Leeds. None of us at school had a football kit and we all needed one to play in. I don't quite know how it happened but we all ended up with Chelsea kits, plain blue with a white stripe down the shorts. I guess London influences must have counted, and to be honest, a plain white kit wasn't too appealing and at the time I barely knew of Leeds. This didn't however result in me supporting Chelsea, not at all, I just needed a kit to play in.

The next thing was that I needed a bag to take my football kit and boots to school in. I remember unwrapping my presents that Christmas and a present from my grandad was a really smart football bag. However it was red, and had Manchester United on it. So here I was, a young boy getting interested in football, living in West London, with a Chelsea football kit, Manchester United football bag, and watching West Ham most Sundays on the tv. I still did not support a specific club, however, and you would have thought that by now something would have had a big enough impact on me to help me make a selection. It never really bothered me. Looking for a club to support wasn't very important at the time.

FANTHOLOGY

Yet with my grandad supporting Fulham, and with Fulham reaching the 1975 Cup Final, things began to get interesting. I remember making Fulham posters for my grandad's car. I would colour black stripes onto white sheets of paper and my grandad taped these up in his car. You would have thought this would have been the start of something but it was not so. Although this was the first Cup Final I had ever watched, and it was quite different watching a whole game, live, and seeing the trophy being presented at the end, it somehow passed by without having too much influence on me. However a few weeks later, another game was to make its mark.

A big deal was being made on radio and tv of a specific football match that was being played that evening. It was the European Cup Final and I was soon aware that Leeds United were playing Bayern Munich. I didn't know quite what the European Cup was all about or how the two teams found themselves in the final, but it was clearly a big occasion, all the talk was about Leeds United and what a big game it was for them. I remember getting carried along by the hype and getting excited about the game and wanting to watch it on tv that night. The problem was that I couldn't be sure I would be allowed to watch it, as my parents didn't have much interest in football and would probably want to watch something else. I'm not quite sure how I swung it, but they said I would allowed me to watch it, so there I sat that evening, in my grandad's football watching chair, with a white scarf, borrowed from my mum, tied around the knob of the chair.

I didn't quite understand all the rules of football, and especially not offside, but I certainly took the injustice of the bad refereeing decisions against Leeds to heart and absorbed the commentator's despair at them. I was quite upset when the final whistle went and

CHOOSING/BEING CHOSEN BY LEEDS

Leeds had lost, and significantly for me, for the first time ever a football result had made an impact on me; it mattered.

You know how they say 'you can't help who you fall in love with' and that it just happens, well that's what happened with me and Leeds. I didn't choose to specifically support them, but that night, it did just happen, that was it. I remember reading the sports pages of the paper the next day and continuing to feel sorry for Leeds and upset at how they had been 'robbed'. I'm sure I must have been influenced by the passion and views at the time of the media but that was definitely it, I was hooked. I had found my club, or rather the club had found me.

Now that I was a Leeds Supporter, I wanted to do it properly and had to have their kit. Yes, I know, before it wasn't too appealing, but now it was a must have. The odds were against me getting it though, what with my mum making such a fuss that she didn't want me having a white kit that would get dirty so quickly and be such a struggle to keep clean. After much pestering however I managed to get my own way and nice, white, football shirt, shorts and socks were purchased. To put the icing on the cake, I also got a badge (the smiley one) and my mum sowed it on the shirt which made it look so much better and really did enhance the Leeds aspect of it. Boy was I chuffed, and I lived in that kit.

It was tough supporting Leeds though, what with all the London influences. I would go to school fetes and find players like Phil Parkes and Don Givens signing autographs. My friends were predominantly QPR supporters, none of them Leeds, and of course, the football coverage on the tv was still heavily biased towards the London clubs. I remained loyal though. The Sunday morning after a Leeds win I would greet the morning newspaper like a lonely dog greeting his owner after coming home from work. By the time my mum and dad got to read the paper, the article on Leeds would always have been carefully cut out and stuck in my scrapbook.

I had a diary where I wrote down all the Leeds results and scorers and if they played an evening game I would listen to my radio secretly in my room, as I should have been asleep, waiting for the football results on Radio 2 after the 10 o'clock news, and write down the score before going to sleep.

Leeds United had become incredibly important to me and I would dedicate my Saturdays to them during the football season. I was very superstitious and would believe that if I had a bad day one day, the next day would always be good. I would therefore always be hoping that something on each Friday would happen to satisfy me that that was a bad day, so that Saturday would subsequently be a good day which could only mean a Leeds win.

I would play keep-up with the ball in the back garden and play mind games. For example, if I kept the ball up ten times, three times in a row, Leeds would win their game, if I didn't they would lose. Of course, if I failed my task I would find an excuse and start again until I reached the right outcome. In a similar vein, I would play the 'Wembley' board game and make my own rules so Leeds would always end up winners. I would often go to swimming club on Saturday mornings and would have rules whereby if I completed a length in a certain number of strokes then Leeds would win, and if not they would lose. Naturally, the rules were made to ensure the outcome of a Leeds win.

My love of Leeds continued from there and led to countless trips around the country and Europe to watch them play. It's such a shame that I just missed out on the Glory Years and Revie era as I have only managed to see Leeds win one trophy, the 1992 League

Championship. I'm so glad I was at Bramall Lane for the Sheffield United game that clinched it.

Obviously I wish for more Leeds success, and the one occasion I really dream of is to watch Leeds in the FA Cup Final. I have had chances to go to one before but have my principles and won't go unless Leeds are playing. The FA Cup Final is a special occasion and one I only want to share with Leeds United and supporters. I want to sing 'Abide With Me' and well up inside, and should we win, cry at the final whistle, and cheer loudly when the cup gets presented and held high by our captain.

Although the team haven't enjoyed the best of times whilst I have been a supporter, it has never crossed my mind to support anyone else. I know I couldn't, it's Leeds or no one. They are the club that have been in my heart and soul since I was a boy and even though none of us can predict the future, this is something I can guarantee will never change.

Mark Walsh

Heir to a King

I was born in a small market town in Leicestershire in May 1957. That was the same month King John was transferred to Juventus for a record fee. Looking back, it seems only right that I should become a follower of Leeds United, the club where he had built his reputation.

My Dad was an Arsenal supporter - because the only shirts they had in a Prisoner of War camp were that colour! But he took me occasionally to watch Leicester City. I can't remember whether it was the '64/65 or '65/66 season, as I was only 6 or 7, but I can remember that the game between Leicester and Leeds was an exciting draw. For some reason, that was it, I was hooked! I didn't want to do what most sons do and support my biggest local team or support one of the main teams their dad did. I wanted to be different - so it was Leeds United for me ...thank you very much. What's more I have never regretted that decision. In fact, as the years pass, I am getting worse in terms of the fanaticism - sad but true!

My son, **LEE D**aniel Shepherd, now follows the team. He did follow his Dad's team and I'm glad as I look forward to going to matches with him, and my daughter Zoe (couldn't get away with **LUCY** - Leeds United Champions of Yorkshire) is a 'secret fan'.

Gary Shepherd

Best Leeds Team whose Surnames Start with 'H'

Harvey, Hird, Hunter, Hart, Hampton, Haaland, Harris, Hodge, Hankin, Hasselbaink, Hendrie.

Subs: Hughes, Haddock, Hawley, Hilaire, Harte, Hibbitt, Halle.

RE

James Lee considers why his trek still has difficulties.

My Journey to Being a Leeds Fan

A newspaper cutting adorns my bedroom wall. It is pinned to a fabric notice board, which is in turn nailed to the wall, within an alcove that harbours my desk. The photo shows Harry Kewell. He looks boyish and vulnerable; he is frozen.

CHOOSING/BEING CHOSEN BY LEEDS

He is frozen in two senses. Firstly, the camera has caught him in mid-step, his right hand cradling a match ball, his left hand hanging limply, gently grazing his white, silken shorts. The middle finger of this left hand is bandaged, surgical tape sheathing a ring, and it points to a number ten. But, far from looking Prime Ministerial, Harry looks scared, the second sense in which he is frozen. The man in front looks tense, but dutiful, the man behind, Eddie Gray, is more dynamic, jogging purposefully up the stairs, avuncular and encouraging. But, as they emerge, up on to the grass of the Ali Sami Yen Stadium, framed by riot police and their shields, with the '99/00 UEFA Cup Semi-Final first leg versus Galatasaray just minutes away, Harry is frozen with fear.

With the sad and senseless murder of two Leeds fans on the night preceding this and with the 'Welcome to Hell' horror of this intimidating football ground as a backdrop, it is understandable for 'H' to be so hesitant, so anxious, so full of dread, even. Although I loathed the event, I treasure this cutting. Just a piece of fading and degrading newspaper, now several years old, but this emotive photo tells a story bigger than itself. And yet, if viewed by the uninitiated, ignorant of the story and untouched by its gravity, Harry Kewell still appears strangely at odds with the role expected of him. He looks less like a professional footballer and more like a human being.

In part, I follow football to feel human, but my relationship with the game is complex. As a child I was confident but socially awkward, I was friendly but a bit pushy and rather smug. I was precocious and enjoyed sensible conversations with adults, probably because my grandad spoke sensibly with me, on our frequent walks around Guiseley and Otley. I was tall and I had a famous dad. These facts - my smugness, my precocity and my parentage - set me apart from my peers and I was, unsurprisingly, not as popular as I could have been. Now 34 and with the pardoning privilege of hindsight, my position as petit pariah was understandable. But, as a nine or ten-year-old I felt lonely and misunderstood.

So, feeling an outcast and longing to be 'one of the lads', I turned to football. I thought that if I played, my peers would accept me or like me even, never mind my inability to actually play. Implausibly, this strategy paid off, at least indirectly.

I genuinely had no natural skill. I was a gangling giraffe or windmill of a boy, a blur of arms and legs. I had no touch, could not read the game and was told I closed my eyes when I got the ball. But, my tactic was simple and direct; if the ball came near me when I was in sight of goal, I would shoot. In this manner I scored ten times for my school team, Green Bottom. Probably my social standing was changed little by this feat, but I *felt* better, more accepted, more normal.

Of course I had been aware of football, and of Leeds United for that matter, for some time. I was familiar with the scarves, the names of certain players, and of the FA Cup. My dad's group The Grumbleweeds had recorded the unmemorable 'String of Beads', to coincide with one of Leeds' cup final appearances. I also knew of something bad called hooliganism. My mum, who was fiercely proud of her ex-rugby league-playing brother, said all football fans were hooligans and all footballers short and somehow unmanly.

All the fuss surrounding football perplexed me but it was with my conscious attempt at social integration through the medium of football that I first became connected with the game. Not yet with Leeds United though. Maybe I was using football for my own ends, as many would become consumers of it in the future. Isn't football sometimes incidental, a vehicle for a social afternoon in the pub, a mock justification for violence? I feel it can be. But at that point in time, with Leeds a fading force and a young boy struggling with his identity, I first became a football fan. It would be several more years before I was a Leeds fan.

So, the murk is clearing as to why my 'relationship with the game is complex'. Still more complex is my relationship with Leeds United. As a youngster, with no family history of physically supporting Leeds, despite that paternal effort to trouble Jimmy Saville's play list, I confess my allegiance lay with another. Like many a football consumer I followed a successful team in red, not Smithy's surrogate club, but the other, who never walk alone and wear shell-suits. Bear with me, this was only a phase.

Then, with my football skills burgeoning and my friendships developing, I was sent, with the passive acceptance of an 11-year-old, to a more 'academic' school. On arrival I learned they didn't play football; rugby was the game, and not the provincial kind. So, thereafter, all I knew of football was distant and spectacular (Espana '82, Mexico '86) or nearby and tragic (Bradford, Hillsborough); and as for Leeds and me, the 80's didn't happen.

But then, 'Ing-ger-land' set the world, and me, in motion. A decade since I had offered myself for selection on the tarmac of a North Leeds Junior School, I was kicking every ball with Gazza et alia in the stadia of Italia '90, albeit from the beery comfort of my local. But this vicarious enjoyment of the World Cup rekindled my interest in football and it coincided with Leeds' belated return to the 'old' First Division. The stage was set for me to realise my destiny. Surely now, no longer needing football as a dating agency for friends, I would ditch my glory-hunting past and support Leeds United, my hometown team. The prodigal son was returning!

The truth is less clear-cut. Of course I thought I was a Leeds fan - I knew the scores and scorers, I could spout second-hand sound bites and punditry. I was saddened by the 5-4 loss to my previous heroes, at least confirming my homecoming, but I didn't go to a single match. Yes, I admired via television the courage of Chapman and the craft of McAllister, the drive of Strachan and the steel of Batty, but I was watching Leeds as I had always watched football - as entertainment. It didn't mean anything. When 'we' finally won the title, I jumped around the lounge, punching the air in celebration. But it was not heartfelt, my reaction was little more than immature triumphalism. Not having stood on the terraces throughout the wilderness years of the '80's, I could not possibly understand the elation, the reaffirmation, the pride felt by lifelong Leeds fans at such a renaissance.

Blissfully unaware at the time of my poor credentials as a fan, the foundations were at least in place. After the Championship of '91/'92, I followed, more closely this time, the next season, with its attendant European campaign. I was thrilled to the point of rapture by the 4-1 crushing of Stuttgart, my genuine heartache at our subsequent exit on away goals then turning to giddy relief at our reinstatement on a technicality. Unusually, I stayed in on the Friday to watch the victorious rematch at an empty Nou Camp. I relished the next round against Rangers, but howled at its outcome. I have no memory of either leg, home or away, save for McAllister's early stunner and Lukic's dazzled mis-punch. Ultimately, the '92/'93 season was a big disappointment, with not a single league win on our travels and a final placing of 17th, but I followed Leeds nonetheless…was I becoming a fan?

CHOOSING/BEING CHOSEN BY LEEDS

I listened regularly to BBC Radio Leeds for the remainder of Howard Wilkinson's tenure and throughout that of George Graham. I watched disbelievingly at tv clips of Tony Yeboah's wonder goals and one afternoon, upon arriving at my parents' home in the Dales, I looked, also in disbelief, at Ceefax. It displayed Leeds Utd 4, Derby County 3 - I had lost radio reception at three nil down!

Then, with the advent of David O'Leary and his 'babies', I finally went to Elland Road. My mate and I bought mini-Season Tickets in the North East Stand. It covered the last eight games of the '98/'99 season, starting rather inauspiciously with the 1-0 defeat to Newcastle but climaxing with Hasselbaink's point blank header against Arsenal. We went on to finish 4th and in the euphoria of the post-match, last-home-game-of-the-season parade it really felt we were destined to achieve something concrete, something beautiful. We had a canny, inspirational manager and a crop of gifted, young players, especially Kewell; we were an exciting, dynamic team and had potential in spades. After this eight-game appetiser, I was ravenous for the start of the next season, which I would watch from the Revie Stand. I was indeed becoming a fan.

The word 'fan' covers a wide spectrum of identities. A colleague of mine, whom I like and respect, has a room in his house full of Leeds memorabilia; programmes, autographs, letters and photos of him with his heroes. It is a shrine to the Whites. He gets to matches before the turnstiles open and he accosts his heroes by the players' entrance. He has little interest in matches not involving Leeds or Leeds players. He is literally fanatical, to an extent bordering on Obsessive Compulsive Disorder.

Thankfully I am not cursed with such pathological fanaticism. However, we all follow Leeds in our own way, as illustrated by this episode, which I remember from my time in the North Stand, the Kop.

Near to my right sat, let's call him Fan A. His behaviour compensated for his bland appearance. He seemed incapable of calm enjoyment. Even during uneventful passages of play he would leap to his feet, wailing unintelligible abuse at the pitch. The frustration and iniquity he felt seemed to stem, not from the match, but from childhood and he indeed screamed like a confused, afflicted toddler. He was a cause of much annoyance, not least to Fan B, sitting two or three rows behind.

Fan B had a scar on his chin and clenched teeth behind unsmiling lips. He reminded me of Clint Eastwood or Robert Mitchum, brooding and menacing. He had had a malevolent eye on the oblivious Fan A for some time and eventually called to him across the intervening rows. He suggested he be more constructive in his support and less of an irritant, or words to that affect. The threat of bodily harm was clear.

But apparently not to Fan A, who foolishly continued in the same annoying manner. So, as assured as a Maitre d', the menacing Fan B enquired as to crybaby A's availability and marched purposefully to the exit. Shocked, speechless and clearly embarrassed, Fan A had no choice but to follow. After, barely 60 seconds, Fan B returned, alone and poker-faced. After ten minutes, Fan A returned sheepishly, his mouth bloodied. He reached across the rows, offering his hand in apology; with his lip swollen, he at least tried to save his face!

This gesture earned Fan A, if not B's respect, at least the right to take up his seat at the next home game, albeit less conspicuously. I rather enjoyed the whole affair - two grown men settling their differences with mild physical violence. This almost wild-west duel seemed reasonable, even moral, and I smile at it now.

These two anecdotes - "Unbalanced fan meets violent fan in tale of Kop justice", and the earlier "Obsessive fan needs therapy" - beg the question: What kind of Leeds fan am I? Well, I'm not unbalanced, violent or obsessive; neither am I cynical, deluded or regretful, nor am I any of the adjectives applicable to the myriad species of Leeds fan. And yet, I have been most of them at one time or another. At the moment I suppose I am a 'fair weather' fan, for I no longer hold a Season Ticket. Some would call me disloyal, traitorous even, but I am comfortable with this position, as I will explain.

Since that joyous, celebratory evening in May 1999 when 'O'Leary's Babies' looked on the verge of greatness, much bad has happened; Galatasaray, that vile 'night on the town', the ill-timed book, the over-ambitious and imprudent spending, the embarrassing sell-off and the inevitable, depressing drop.

Mixed with anger and disappointment, my prevailing emotion on these matters has been a feeling of loss, the loss of a glimpsed at but unrealised future. Feeling betrayed by the club I loved and with no masochistic appetite for further disappointment, I stopped going. I will go again, one day, but after four and a half unforgettable seasons, I'm taking a break from Leeds United. Like others in this story, I'm only human.

I used to wonder what might have been if the club had been managed differently, but I know such navel gazing is futile and childish. More recently I have, instead, come to cherish the happy memories of the last five seasons; two truly epic European adventures, intense Premiership rivalry. Okay, we didn't win anything, but few clubs do.

Actually, I am philosophical of our current plight. Failure and perceived injustice are as much a part of football as are hat tricks and trophies. So too are acquisitive agents, tabloid-style indiscretions, disloyal players and incompetent referees. I believe one should embrace football in all its grisly detail. An acceptance of such horrors makes being a fan more entertaining and, in Leeds' case, more tolerable.

And what of Harry Kewell? The newspaper cutting, of which he is central, will retain its place on my wall and in my heart, but he long since left my affections. In leaving Leeds, Kewell became the very epitome of the modern day, professional footballer - cold and greedy. Ironic indeed, considering my earlier comment on his humanity! As an impressionable youngster I flirted with Liverpool, as I have confessed, so maybe I'm no better. The difference is that I came back, just as Batty did, just as Deane has, albeit of necessity, and just as one day Smith might. Kewell, however, will forever 'walk alone'.

So, initially I wasn't a Leeds fan and then I became one. Fake at first, and then genuine. Now I'm a disaffected, nostalgic Leeds fan, but soon I'll be more attentive and hopeful. Eventually, I'll be a celebratory Leeds fan, with my team and I 'marching on together'. My journey continues.

James Lee, from Leeds, Leeds fan

United's England internationals versus the Rest of Britain

ENGLAND: Martyn; Reaney, Charlton, Hunter, Cooper; Willis Edwards, Currie, Madeley: Clarke, Jones, O'Grady.

England Subs: Seaman, Sproston, Woodgate, Hodge, Fowler.

REST OF BRITAIN: Harvey; Kelly, O'Leary, McQueen, Gray F; Strachan, Giles, Collins; Bremner, Charles, Gray E.

Rest of Britain Subs: Sprake, Stevenson, McAllister, Lorimer, Jordan.

GG

In contrast to James, there were no such difficulties for supporters like Danny...

Why Leeds?

A Sicilian father, an Italian mother and dragged up in the heart of Chapeltown, a mainly black and Asian area of Leeds; hardly inevitable that one would become a Leeds fan. Ah, but then I forgot to mention that I was born in Jimmy's, a hospital wherein no child is released into the community until their parents have signed an allegiance agreement to Leeds United.

Despite this, when one bears in mind the built-in, some might say almost primeval, tribal, desire within all fathers to direct their children towards a certain team, it would have been quite possible that I'd have ended up following the likes of Juventus, which was my father's team. Only quite possible though... any attempt to actually see this through would have resulted in an awful lot of baiting and schoolyard fights. Well, there's only so much pizza-related name calling that a young first-generation immigrant can take before threatening to call in the boys. 'The boys' were my two other Italian friends, can't remember their names, Quattro Formaggio or Mozzarella or something...

Having become a father several years ago, I understand all too well the unnecessary, and often unwelcome, pressures that a dad can put on his children to try and steer them towards following a certain team. Well, his team to be precise. I, for instance, lie constantly to my children concerning the successes of Leeds United.

When I arrive home after a game, my young children will greet me excitedly waiting to find out whether Leeds have won. 'Of course they did - they scored loads and loads of goals.' Or 'lurds and lurds' of goals, if I have slipped back into my Leeds accent after an afternoon of West Yorkshire chanting. Now, in recent times that hasn't exactly been true. Goals have been few and far between and Leeds' success has become a bit of an oxymoron, but that hasn't prevented me from embellishing the truth slightly to make Leeds United sound more of an attractive proposition. Having sent my children to a Catholic school, I am aware of how beneficial a religious endorsement can be, so is it wrong to use it as a method to engineer loyalties? My eldest daughter came to me and one day asked why Leeds are the best team in the world. Remember she is under the misapprehension that they win every game... Seeing a valuable opportunity for assimilation, I embarked on another unsubstantiated claim. This conversation actually happened:

'Daddy, why are Leeds the best team in the world?'

'Well darling, I'm glad you asked.' (That's me by the way). I continued, 'Can you tell me what colour Leeds play in?'

'White, Daddy.'

'Excellent. Now, when you are at school and you draw pictures of Jesus and of God, what are they wearing?'

'Long clothes, Daddy.'

'Good, good. Now, what colour are those clothes?'

'White!'

'Well there you have it. Leeds wear God's colours. They are God's own team - he wants them to win. That is why they are the best.'

I then retired to take in the wonderful scene I had created. The fact that I didn't consider the ramifications of such a comment, or the ability of my daughter to progress the thinking further is neither here nor there. Neither is the fact that at the next parent-teacher meeting, her form teacher asked my wife why my daughter had told her that, 'If you liked any other team than Leeds, you were sinning against God as they were all the Devil's teams.' Some people can be so touchy I thought, about my wife, as she explained her disappointment in my child rearing techniques.

So what does all this tell us? Well it tells us how it is, or was for me. You're from Leeds, you live in Leeds, you go to school in Leeds. You ARE Leeds. The interesting question is where does being Leeds take you? Well it finally took me to Elland Road. I could never get my father to take me, he loved football, but had remained indifferent towards Leeds United since his arrival in Yorkshire in the early 1950s. My only hope was my elder brothers. They would go to games, and I was desperate to follow them but my over possessive Italian mother insisted that it was far too dangerous for a young boy. And anyway I had my cousins I could play with. Who were girls! I mean, I ask you! I resolved this with a certain amount of guile, technique and subterfuge. I threw a tantrum.

You can be standing in a supermarket (most commonly Aldi) - and little Wayne will suddenly throw a wobbler because he can't have the red Power Ranger that is holding the tube of sweets. He's on his back, he's kicking his legs - you want to run him over with your trolley and he's screaming loud enough to make your ears bleed. Amateur! The tantrum I threw was measurable on the Richter scale. The tantrum I threw became folklore in the suburbs of Leeds. The tantrum I threw resulted in several clips round the ear but also resulted in me going to Leeds v West Ham, 9.3.1976, we drew 1-1, Joe Jordan scored.

I knew where I wanted to stand. I'd heard all the other boys at school talk about the parts of the ground, and I had already made up my mind up. I wanted to be in the Kop. That's where my schoolmates would be and in the hope that I might gain some cred by being seen at a match, that's where I was heading. And with that, I was told, 'Shut up you little sod, we're going to the Lowfields.' I was just short of nine. My bigger and older brothers were not to be trifled with.

I accepted my lot and consoled myself with the fact that if I sang long and hard enough then maybe my friends would be able to pick me out, maybe all the Lowfielders around me would stop and commend me on my vocal commitment. Maybe Billy Bremner or even our Lord Eddie Gray would feel the need to come over and personally show his appreciation for a level of support the likes of which they've never seen in all their years at Elland Road. I've never been short of imagination. Friends, yes: imagination, no.

CHOOSING/BEING CHOSEN BY LEEDS

There are times in individuals' lives when a set of circumstances and events collide to make the perfect moment. Some people believe it is when their children are born, some believe it is their first kiss, some even believe it might be their wedding day. Idiots the lot of them. None of them compare to how I felt at my first game. I've been to many important games since then, Play-Off finals, FA Cup semi finals, promotion-clinching matches etc. All are fabulous memories in their own right, but it is your first ever game that helps you make sense of it all.

At your first game, results don't matter. I know the West Ham result but simply because I have spent time finding it out. I can't remember the performances, I can't remember the line-up. I can remember paying at the turnstile and being pushed through with my brother shouting at me to stand still until he got through. Only season ticket holders had advance tickets for league games in those days. I remember walking past the Gents' thinking that I might get washed away in the tide of what was coming back out through the entrance. I remember my brothers, each with their hands against my back ushering me up towards the terrace. And I remember the pitch. The huge expanse of green, that even after nearly a whole season of play and northern weather, looked soft, flat and smooth. I remember the huge towering floodlights at each corner of the ground, about which every newbie was told, 'They're the tallest in Europe you know.' All of it was a rite of passage.

It's not about being hooked. You're already hooked. It's not about knowing all the stats. I used to spend hours regurgitating player and team stats without ever having seen a game. It's not even about having a full Panini Sticker album, no matter what Andrew Clarke tells you, although those foil team badges were really cool. You can follow a team, you can fill in your pullout wall-chart, but it's actually being there that really counts. The day I finally went to see

Leeds United, even if I had never got to see them again, was the time that I suddenly understood Why Leeds? Because me and 35,000 other people wanted it to be. We ARE Leeds.

Danny Martorana

... or youngsters like Chris.

100% Leeds

My name is Chris Payne, I'm 13 and from Southampton. I've always supported Leeds and so has my dad. I go to watch as many Leeds games as I can.

The reasons I am a Leeds fan are because we are the greatest club, we have the best fans, the best atmosphere and every fan is 100% Leeds. I LOVE LEEDS UNITED.

Chris Payne

And Tom...

Why I support Leeds United

The reason I have always supported Leeds United is, quite simply, because my dad does. And he started because of his dad. It just seems the proper thing to do. Virtually everyone I know supports their team because of their parent or parents.

My earliest memory of the Mighty Whites is, in fact, their 2-0 defeat to Liverpool at Elland Road in the '94/'95 season when I was only four. I remember Nigel Martyn, our recent signing from Crystal Palace, getting outrun by Steve McManaman, who slid the ball into the Kop end's net.

CHOOSING/BEING CHOSEN BY LEEDS

What keeps me going every other Saturday, making the one and half hour journey from Ripley to Leeds, is the excitement, the tension, the cheering and jeering, but most of all my love for the beautiful game.

Apart from the obvious reasons, I felt most let down in the dreadful 'relegation season' not because of the bad team performances but because of the fact that I couldn't get the adrenalin rush each time we scored. I felt what was the point of bothering because that is what most of the players seemed to believe as well.

There's something really addictive, though, about Leeds United and football in general. Personally, I can't get enough of it and, whatever happens, I'll be back for more.

Tom Holmes (13)

... and Amy.

Team Spirit

Hi, my name is Amy, I'm 13 and I come from Ossett, West Yorkshire. I support LEEDS because, as well as being Yorkshire's no.1 football team, we have the WORLD's best TEAM SPIRIT and nothing can ever change that.

Being a life long Leeds supporter and recent season ticket holder, I've stuck with Leeds through all our ups and downs to see the fans crying with happiness or after our defeat against Bolton leading us to relegation, crying with misery. Despite this, at the last home game against Charlton, we did what only Leeds fans could do at such a time and invaded the pitch with the words, "We're going down, but we'll be back! WE ARE LEEDS!"

This amazing devotion and our great history of a winning team is why I am PROUD to be a Leeds fan and I'm sure people from all over the world can say the same.

I even illustrated my pride live on Radio Aire. I declared, 'They can take away our place in the Premiership, they can take away our star players, but they can NEVER take away our team spirit! We are LEEDS and we are PROUD!'

And that is why I am proud to support Leeds United!

Amy Higgott

Reporting on politics has taken him away from his native county but the final contributor to this section still holds Leeds United close to his heart. Following them was hardly a matter of choice.

A Choice of One

Growing up in Ilkley in the late 60's and early 70's, who else would you support?

James Hardy,
BBC Political Correspondent

Chapter 2

Loyalty: Marching on Together

All the effort and cost of following Leeds. What are the reasons? What are the rewards?

Ray Fell is Chairman of Leeds United Supporters' Club and has followed his hometown team for nearly sixty years.

I first watched Leeds United in the season following World War II, 1946/47. At that time, being a South Leeds lad and having attended a rugby playing school, my loyalties were shared with Hunslet Rugby League Club.

I have little recollection of individual games in that first season but I well remember my favourite player being Gerald Henry who had the reputation of being a hard player. The team then was riddled with players whose surname started with H; Hodgson, Holley, Henry, Hindle and Heaton. The season itself was a disaster and Leeds were relegated to the Second Division with a record low number of points. There were some brighter notes though, like a home game against Middlesbrough (on Christmas Day!) when, with around fifteen minutes to go we were 3-0 down and many of us were heading for the terrace exits. A roar turned our heads as Leeds managed to score. Excitement then rapidly increased as we made it 2-3 and we talked for years after of the final score of 3-3, having managed to equalise.

Leeds United in the late forties were mediocre, a mid-table Division Two side. We had players who raised the temperature but only for a short time; players like Albert Wakefield who scored 21 goals in season 1947/48 but failed to produce the following year and promptly departed, remembered for spending more time on his backside than on his feet. There was Flight Lieutenant Ken Chisholm, too. Like some of the other players he'd head for home matches by tram car, along with the fans. But, amid stories of fall outs with Manager Major Buckley, Chisholm would make for The Peacock pub before going to the actual dressing room.

I remember the 1948 cup tie away to Blackpool. Our local newspaper, the Yorkshire Evening News I think it was, ran the headline 'GADSBY TO MARK MATTHEWS'. I remember my father saying, 'If anyone can mark Stanley Matthews, Gadsby can.' Leeds lost 4-0 and by the looks of it Gadsby never got close to the great Stan.

1948/49 saw new players join the club: goal scorers Len Browning, Ray Iggleden and Jim McMorran. Later that season there arrived another new face, a player who not only got the fans talking at the time but ever since, too. That player was, of course, John Charles. He played three games that season but by the following term Leeds fans knew they now had something special in the team.

To those of us lucky enough to see him arrive and develop, he will always be remembered as THE all time great.

In those days I couldn't travel to many away games yet I have fond memories of the replayed FA Cup Fourth Round tie at Bolton. I was working as a young office boy at Wm Moorhouse & Son in Old Lane, Beeston at the time. The Moorhouse family were keen Leeds fans and that afternoon they had me parade round the factory with notices relaying the latest state of play. The final score was Bolton 2, Leeds 3 and the cheers of everyone in the factory made it a day to remember. The team during those giddy days was memorable for me too. We had the half-back line of Burden (captain), Charles and Kerfoot. Kerfoot was cup tied that season but Irish international James McCabe adequately replaced him. Frank Dudley had joined Leeds as well and we had an excellent goalkeeper in Harold Searson. Our full backs were pretty useful too; Jimmy Milburn and Jimmy Dunn, Dunn being hailed as the best Scottish full back never to be capped by his country and a sliding tackler of perfection. In that season John Charles played all his games at centre half, scoring just three goals.

The following season saw us finish mid-table again but it was still a better time generally and we had a better team than before. The highlight was the beginning of John Charles as centre forward. The records show that he played twenty eight games up front, scoring twenty six goals. The arguments as to John's best position - in defence or in attack - commenced and remain a matter for debate even to this day. Goals speak louder than defensive tackles and headers though and 1953/4 witnessed his goal scoring achievement which I think will last forever. John Charles scored forty-two goals for Leeds United that season.

Another personal record took place then too: one of my favourite inside forwards, Albert Nightingale, scored seventeen goals as well as creating many of Charles's. It was rumoured that if you tackled Nightingale within twenty-five yards of the penalty box you risked giving away a penalty kick, such was Albert's fond reputation but there was much more to his game - in those days of pure football he was a genuine class act.

Harold Brook came from Sheffield United and the baptism of a young Jack Charlton took place. The arrival of these two players led to the success we'd longed for. Charlton took Charles's centre half spot, allowing John to move up front regularly and score twenty nine goals. Brook scored a good sixteen while Nightingale chipped in with a very useful ten. Raich Carter was Manager and that '55/56 season of promotion was one to really cherish.

The new season in the top division started off with mixed emotions. A 5-1 win over Everton was marred by Albert Nightingale being carried off with an injury which would put an end to his football career. John Charles of course carried on where he'd left off, scoring thirty-eight goals this time around. Leeds finished our highest ever then position of eighth in Division One. As I say, the memories of that season are not all good though. As well as losing our second most important player, the South Stand (now the west side of the stadium) burned down and the Board needed to sell John Charles to Juventus to pay for its rebuilding. The fee was a then world record but all Juventus fans knew they'd got a bargain, John went on to break Italian records and he's still regarded as the best ever foreign player to appear for them.

Of all my Leeds United memories, the privilege of having seen John Charles appear for us, as well as later knowing the man personally, ranks very high. I know I shall never see his equal.

Fortunes faltered for the team and we soon ended up back in Division Two. In fact, in 1961/62 we looked likely contenders for the Third Division and finally finished nineteenth! That season though, also witnessed the arrival of a young Billy Bremner, a small copper-topped Scot who looked too slow to be a winger and also was often, so we heard, homesick for his birthplace of Stirling. Our player-manager at the time was an England international no less: one Don Revie. He'd been appointed by Harry Reynolds, the chairman who used to amuse fans during half-time intervals with predictions that Leeds United would not only win the Second Division but also Division One and the domestic cups as well as whatever Europe had to offer! The fans' ensuing laughter echoed around the ground. But later that season, one Bobby Collins joined...

Other arrivals proved important too: speedy Don Weston and a young, black South African 'wizard' Albert Johanneson who soon became a favourite of the Leeds supporters. Jim Storrie was another highly relevant player, scoring many vital goals. The 1964/65 season put a stop to the laughter as Reynolds proved his point. Back in Division One again, the club awakened the nation to the 'birth' of a new Leeds United - and there are many who never forgave us for it. We finished a very creditable second place - on goal difference - and had the added bonus of our first ever Wembley final appearance. I shall never forget the FA Cup Semi Final at Nottingham Forest's ground versus Man U, particularly seeing Billy's red head rise above all the six footers there to flick the winner in to the net. We lost the Cup Final to Liverpool, deservedly so, 2-1, but it was a season that would change the history of Leeds United and possibly the city itself. The fans had become true believers.

The great Don Revie era between 1964 and 1974 is well recorded and has been written about from all angles possible - even Monty Python! His team not only became household names, they honoured Don himself too, as well as the city and the Leeds supporters. The League Championship was won twice, the FA Cup and League Cup once and two victories in the Fairs' (UEFA) Cup. There wasn't a season when Leeds weren't challenging for honours on at least three or four fronts. Their failure to win even more trophies was due to their own success: too many games with too short intervals between, usually at the end of yet another packed season. Few other clubs had to put up with that problem and, despite what some might claim, conditions and circumstances were much harder in those days than they are nowadays. Any disappointments over that era are easily erased with the memories of the great Super Leeds team and the excellent entertainment provided by Leeds United on the field of play.

I'm truly grateful that my position with Leeds United Supporters' Club has given me the opportunity to know the members of that great team and to mourn the loss of those now sadly departed. I'm deeply thankful too to have known Don Revie for the man he was. His wife Elsie is still a friend to my wife and I, and she still loves the club. She has great pride in being the President of Leeds United Supporters' Club.

Following Don's resignation in 1974 we had the short reign of Brian Clough, and that's the kindest thing I can say about it! Jock Stein followed, accepting the job while knowing that he would grab the Scotland job if, as forecast, it was offered to him. It was and so again we had a humiliatingly short reign to deal with. The Board finally got it right in my opinion when they appointed Jimmy Armfield as Manager. He stepped in and stopped the rot, taking us to a respectable ninth place while basically trying his best to overhaul the place. Armfield deserves credit too for getting us to the European Cup Final in 1975. That May day was memorable for just the occasion but instantly forgettable too for the behaviour of some of the fans, not all, and certainly not the majority, who disgraced the occasion and brought a heavy penalty on to the club with European disqualification.

The 1980's brought a succession of ex-Leeds players who tried hard to make their mark as manager. Each one loved the club and each had the backing and best wishes of success from the fans.

Allan Clarke had the misfortune of taking Leeds in to the Second Division while his successor Eddie Gray looked to have found the right formula when he fielded a young and talented team. Unfortunately the players never quite brought it off and most eventually found their success elsewhere. The third ex-player to try as Leeds manager was of course Billy Bremner.

With respect to Allan and Eddie, I believe the fans possibly wanted success even more for Billy than for they. In spite of one memorable season when he came within a cat's whisker of achieving a Cup Final and promotion 'double', it was not to be. You had to feel for him during that FA Cup Semi Final defeat against Coventry and losing to Charlton in the Play Off Final. The following season, yet another disappointment for all Leeds United people, Billy Bremner suffered the fate of all managers when success eludes them.

Howard Wilkinson took over, bringing with him cynical media comment that he was unable to take a football club that extra distance on to real success. Wilkinson was a real planner, he knew instinctively what was needed, first to actually save Leeds from the Third Division and then to take us forward, both on and off the field. He bought astutely and brought in some great players, some of whom would have great influence on the future of the team. Men like Gordon Strachan and Vinnie Jones rarely, if ever, let anyone down at the club.

Howard not only won promotion to Division One again, he won the Championship too, becoming only the second Leeds manager in history to bring a trophy to Elland Road and the second to take us to a major final at Wembley. And he fostered the idea of, and put in to real practice, the Youth Academy. The quality youngsters his regime developed benefited consequent managers George

Graham and David O'Leary and we should remember that the fees some of those players have raised for the club did help to restore a little sanity to the financial situation, tragic though their sales were.

I have found it hard to enjoy the times since Howard Wilkinson departed. There have certainly been good times and we seemed to be winning friends and to be nearing success again. But the horrors of Istanbul, the disgraces of events in Leeds city centre, the writing of books and most of all the mismanagement of a great club have deeply taken their toll. The damage done to a great club and the pain it has caused the world's best supporters is all quite unforgivable. I sincerely hope that Gerald Krasner and his Directors can restore financial normality to the club because when the chips were down and we were going under they were the only ones in this rich and booming city to come up with the goods and come to the rescue.

And the loyalty and support of the countless Leeds United fans across the planet deserves far better, both on the pitch and from the media.

Ray Fell

Leeds Player Names / Film Star etc Names

PUKKA - part 1

Mick / Alan	BATES
Willie / Tom	BELL
Billy / Euan	BREMNER
Michael / Jeff	BRIDGES
Tomas / James	BROLIN

LOYALTY: MARCHING ON TOGETHER

Kenny / George   BURNS
Bobby / Joan   COLLINS
Terry / Gary   COOPER
Alan / Tony   CURTIS
Mervyn / Doris   DAY
Martin / Angie   DICKINSON

RE

Que Sera Sera, Leeds Style

Unlike many supporters mine was not an instant love affair with Leeds United. There was no cupid's arrow or bolt of lightning on my first few visits to the ground. My debut at Elland Road was as a 10 year old along with three of my cousins, the eldest of them being the grand old age of 12. Even in the modern day climate of peace and goodwill to all men, what parent would let their child of such a tender age venture to Elland Road, especially when Newcastle Utd were the visitors?

My 'streetwise' cousins had persuaded my mam it would be safe (didn't she read the newspapers?!) and as we lived on Wesley Street I was actually only 200 yards down the road.

We got into the ground early and took up a position on the wall of the walkway which separated the Lowfields terrace and seats. As I remember, the game was an unspectacular draw with Allan Clarke and John Tudor scoring the goals. My abiding memory of this match was the sporadic attempts by lone Geordies to get from the Scratching Shed to the Kop, and my cousin Tish having his scarf nicked by some young Leeds fan who had offered to show us the best way out of the ground five minutes from time.

FANTHOLOGY

I have to admit to being impressed by the big crowd but the atmosphere didn't really grab me. I felt like an outsider looking in. My cousins knew all the songs and were really wrapped up in the whole thing, for me it was okay but nothing to compare with my true passion - watching New Hunslet over the road at the Greyhound Stadium; now that was excitement!

It was a few years before I went again and saw a match whose significance was lost on me at the time. This was the 3-2 classic with our archenemies from across the Pennines. What more could the game offer me - a night match atmosphere, Jock Stein on the brink of leaving, the return of Jordan and McQueen - two 'Judases' for the price of one? I was at the back of the Kop for this one, not a pleasant experience for a four-foot-nothing little lad like me. Again I couldn't get into the frenzied atmosphere that surrounded me. Though it shames me to say it, at 3-2 I was praying for no more goals, I was in fear of being trampled to death with the crush that would have followed an equaliser

A few other forgettable matches followed but it was five years later in 1982 that it finally happened. The thunderbolt hit and the love affair began. It was the last home game of the season against Brighton, a match in which we needed two points (or so we thought) to avoid relegation. At half time we were one nil down, Michael Robinson celebrating their goal by running the length of the West Stand with his thumb down (what a reptile!). As the teams went off you could sense the crowd had lost all hope. Then it happened, a moment of sheer inspiration by the PA announcer as he put on some of the classic "old" Leeds records - 'Glory Glory' and 'Marching on Together'. The crowd picked up on this and soon the whole ground was belting out the anthems, even me. I was so wrapped up in the emotion of it all that I hadn't realised the teams had come back out and the match was once again underway.

Soon we'd got it back to 1-1 then 2-1, the place erupted - we'd stayed up. I was then involved in my first ever pitch invasion. FANTASTIC.

Fuelled with the euphoria of "arriving" as a true fan I sprinted up Wesley Street to see if I could see myself on Grandstand. It was here I was brought down to earth with a bump when my dad informed me of other results which meant the win wasn't good enough, we now had to at least draw at West Brom in midweek to survive.

The whole country seemed to be celebrating when we went down and having a laugh at our expense (sounds familiar). For me, as with many other fans, it only strengthened our resolve and commitment to the club.

The consequent "dark years" weren't that bad for me; sure I knew the history of this great club but I was never really a part of the Glory Years. It's all relative and a good result coupled with a great atmosphere was all that mattered. The fact it was against the likes of Grimsby or Carlisle as opposed to Arsenal or Liverpool was of no consequence to me. There were some great times in the Second Division and even though gates had dwindled to 16,000 a visit to Elland Road was always an event. The lack of visiting support didn't dampen the atmosphere as the Leeds fans would generate (friendly) rivalry between themselves: 'Gelderd End v South Stand', 'Celtic v Rangers', 'TISWAS v Swap Shop', anything to take our minds off the substandard football.

I didn't venture to many away matches, the only excuse I can give is that I'm not that tough and the thought of being chased round Hull or Barnsley town centre didn't really appeal to me. I don't know if I was some kind of jinx but most of the ones I did attend usually ended in a riot of some description.

FANTHOLOGY

The worst by far was the visit to St Andrews on the final day of the '84/'85 season. Birmingham were already promoted and Leeds still had a mathematical chance of joining them should a 101 other results go our way. About 10,000 optimistic Leeds fans made the trip and from the time we parked up near the ground you could sense an evil atmosphere in the air. Fans of both clubs, and not a small minority, did not cover themselves in glory that day. A young fan died when a wall collapsed, this shouldn't happen at football. But for the horrific events unfolding in Bradford, which took away the media attention, we could have found ourselves expelled from the league.

Another event that deeply affected me that day (and looking back it holds absolutely no significance in comparison to the deaths of so many fans) was the treatment of Eddie Gray by so called Leeds fans. When Eddie came out to try and calm the troublesome supporters he was met with a hail of missiles from the Leeds end. All he could do was shake his head and walk dejectedly away. I couldn't believe what I had witnessed. Weeks later stories were going round that this was the work of Chelsea fans who had come to join up with Leeds to fight the Birmingham 'Zulus'.

Whether there is any truth in this is neither here nor there, it was all I needed to exonerate the Leeds fans and increase my hatred for Chelsea. It was only years later I came to appreciate that Chelsea weren't our number one enemy, I'll go as far to say I mellowed towards them slightly (well the club rather than the fans) when they had the fabulous Zola in their ranks.

The release for my hatred of all things blue was to pen a tongue in cheek song that would have my mates in fits of laughter in the pub before matches. It's my pride and joy that the song went on to become a terrace classic, and has been adapted by fans of other clubs up and down the country. Lennon has 'Imagine', Robbie has 'Angels', Peter Andre 'Insania' and me - Hodge - I've got my 'Doris Day Remix: When I was just a little boy…'

The version of the song that made its way to the terraces and is still there is not exactly as my original. The last lines of my original were the more contrived 'Go get your father's gun, and shoot the Chelsea scum. Leeds are number one'. The last line has been replaced by a repeat of 'Shoot the Chelsea scum' followed by the addition of 'We hate Chelsea, We hate Chelsea.'

I don't disagree with it, the re-mix is far punchier!

I can't take total credit for the song though, it was a bunch of lads I stood with on the Kop who ensured it got maximum air play at away matches where it was easier to get new things going. So Frankie, Owen, Dan, Hill and the rest of the Little Park gang, take a well deserved bow.

The dark years seemed to go on forever and while Sgt Wilko quite rightly receives the accolades for making us a major force in English football again we shouldn't underestimate the impact the '86/'87 season had on our return to the big time. This was the season when Billy Bremner's team reached the Play-Off Final and FA Cup Semi-Final. To me this was the season that showed the real potential of Leeds United. Crowds increased as the season progressed and the 31,000 for the QPR cup tie was the biggest at Elland Road for many a year. It's hard to get excited about that size of attendance these days but this was the pre-Gazzamania era when gates at football were well down. I remember wondering on the walk home, still catching my breath from seeing Brendan Ormsby score the winner, if I'd ever get to be part of such a big crowd and electrifying atmosphere again.

And there lies one beauty of Leeds: just when you think it can't get any better, it does.

Those fans who stayed loyal through the Second Division last time know that even in the darkest days it was still great to be a Leeds fan. Those are the fans who really appreciated the '92 Championship and more recently the march across Europe. The new generation of fans who are experiencing life outside the Premiership for the first time should enjoy the ride - there's going to be one hell of a party a few years from now.

Hodge

Although it is often said there are more important things in life than football, here the two are movingly interlinked.

Football and Illness, you know

The doctor sits and says to me, 'I'm sorry, you've got the big bad 'C'.'
I sit there in a state of shock,
time running down on my internal clock.
Scared now, I start to cry. Will I live or will I die?

Doctor says, 'It's not too late.' They'll give me drugs or operate.
X-rays, drugs it has to be - the less intrusive course for me.

Weeks later in a hospital bed,
into my arm the drugs are fed.

LOYALTY: MARCHING ON TOGETHER

I'm feeling sick, don't know what to do,
but then there's always someone worse than you.

Start reading the paper, always begin at the back.
What's this? LEEDS UNITED UNDER ATTACK!
Another paper, for another angle,
it's money problems the club can't wrangle.
The team I've supported Man and Boy,
people now hunger to destroy.

A Cancer's eating away at my club,
a sickness, a topic for men down the pub.
There's specialists offering ways to amend
the downward curve of what seems like our end.

Now we're fighting on together.
Linked, desperate to be free,
beating shocks to our systems
LEEDS UNITED AND ME!

David Barker

Bremner, Bankruptcy and Beyond:

My love affair with football started relatively late. I have no memory of the beautiful game prior to starting school but that is hardly surprising for a kid brought up on a small farm in the North East of Scotland in the early Sixties. We had a black and white tv and, hard as it may be to imagine in these days of wall-to-wall coverage of football, back then there was little or none televised. It was only when I started school in 1963 and moved from the farm into my home town of Inverurie that I discovered football, both the joy of playing as well as the joy of watching top-class football.

FANTHOLOGY

Being a Scot my first football allegiances were north of the border - Celtic and the Scottish national team. Like most Scottish kids, I also followed an English team. And it was only natural that my team south of the border should be Leeds United. Why natural? Leeds United had just come to prominence under Don Revie and, of course, the core of the team was Scottish led by my all-time football hero, Billy Bremner. Billy embodied the Scottish attitude to football - a never-say-die passion for the game and a flair to excite and entertain. Billy supported Celtic as a kid and captained Leeds United and Scotland. If Celtic, Leeds United and Scotland were good enough for Billy Bremner, they were good enough for Billy Gerrard.

So from the late Sixties onwards I followed Leeds United from afar. The brilliance of the team more than anything was summed up by the legendary display of keep-ball against Southampton. I love players with flair and the great Revie team had it in spades. And, of course, my other massive favourite was Eddie Gray, one of the truly great Scottish wingers with an amazing ability to beat defenders with pure skill and trickery. My other Leeds memories, like so many of my Tartan Army memories, are of disappointments - the 1970 FA Cup Final replay, the offside goal by West Brom that robbed Leeds of the League Championship in 1971, the 1975 European Cup Final and relegation from Division One.

It was preordained that I should end up moving to Leeds to live and work. I took a lectureship at the University of Leeds in September 1984 and I've remained in Leeds ever since. I wouldn't move anywhere else in England. My daughters are Leeds-born and have been brought up to be proud of their home town team, Leeds United, as well as their Scottish parentage. I knew Leeds United was big but I didn't realise just how big until I moved to Yorkshire. Living in Morley, I drive by Elland Road and the Billy Bremner statue every day. I get a buzz every time I do so. Leeds United is my team and I'm proud of it.

I stopped playing Saturday football in 1996 and became a season ticket-holder in the Upper East Stand. By coincidence my regular attendance at Elland Road started just as Leeds United was bought by Caspian plc (soon to be renamed Leeds Sporting plc) and became a listed company with shares traded on the London Stock Exchange. I subsequently bought 6,000 shares as a further emotional investment in my team.

The first season was transitional. George Graham came in, strengthened the defence so that we didn't leak goals and ensured mid-table security. We then moved on the next season with the astute purchase of the then unknown Hasselbaink to add attacking flair to defensive organisation. Kewell also emerged as a real prospect from the football academy. We were on a roll and qualification for the UEFA Cup was achieved. I followed Leeds United both home and away that season, missing only a handful of games.

For season 1998/99 I invested in both home and away season tickets and went to every game from the Carlsberg Trophy pre-season tournament in Dublin to Madeira and Rome. The most expensive day trip wasn't Madeira or Rome but Leicester away mid-week in the League Cup. I had a business meeting in Glasgow that day so it was a case of getting up early morning to drive to East Midlands airport to fly to Glasgow, getting back at 6pm and driving to Filbert Street. All was going well until we conceded two late goals. It was a long journey back up the M1 that night.

FANTHOLOGY

Our first away game in Europe that season was a strange affair. There was intense press speculation that Graham was about to jump ship and move back to North London to manage Spurs. Before kick-off Peter Ridsdale came over to the fans to tell us that Graham would be resigning the next day. Not surprisingly when Graham emerged from the tunnel leading the team out he was greeted by boos from the Leeds fans. The locals looked bewildered. I always wondered what the Leeds players thought of the reception. It turned out to be a real struggle that night with Leeds losing the game and going through after a penalty shoot-out. Maybe in retrospect Peter Ridsdale might have been better advised not have to told us until after the match about Graham's impending departure.

Every cloud has a silver lining. Graham's departure opened the way for O'Leary and Gray to take control of team affairs and the rest as they say is history. O'Leary gave the youngsters their head and produced a team of flair and dynamism that made all Leeds fans proud. Back-to-back European semi-finals returned the glory days to Elland Road and gave us some great European nights. Who can forget our last-minute rain-soaked victory over AC Milan, our demolition of Besiktas or the struggle to hold on to our lead against Barcelona until the fourth minute of injury time? Family commitments limited my own away travels during our European adventures but I remember the many stories from fellow fans of their trips across Europe.

But, as seemingly is always the case with Leeds United, our successes also involved disappointments and tragedy. The murder of two of our fans in Istanbul deeply affected all Leeds fans as the tributes outside Elland Road testified. The infamous events outside the Majestyk nightclub in January 2000 and the subsequent court cases cast a long, dark shadow over the club, besmirching its good name and allowed the London-based media to wage an anti-Leeds campaign reminiscent of the Revie era. And ultimately the football team suffered. I remain convinced that the squad we had at the start of the 2001/02 season should have won the Premiership. We had a great opportunity in October to put some clear water between ourselves and the other leading teams but successive draws against Liverpool, Chelsea and Manchester United, all games we should and could have won, kept us in the pack. We then had three very winnable home games within six days in December but these games yielded only four points with the 4-3 defeat by Newcastle United after leading 3-1 being particularly hard to take. Although we went top of the Premiership on New Year's Day the writing was on the wall. The fall out of the court case, the growing financial problems, rumoured frictions within the dressing room and between chairman and manager, all contributed to a downward spiral that ultimately took us out of Europe and eventually out of the Premiership.

Relegation was painful even more so after the recent glories. I went to the Reebok Stadium to witness the final rites. The collapse after going ahead early summed up our season. Despite Eddie Gray's valiant efforts to motivate a squad decimated by enforced transfers and mismanagement, we were ultimately found to be wanting at the highest level. The league table doesn't lie. We just were not good enough over the entire season. It is so ironic that our defeat at Bolton was exactly three years to the day that we had played Valencia in the Champions' League Semi Finals. From the top four in Europe to the bottom three in the Premiership in three short years. And now we find ourselves in the most competitive football league in Europe. Every match in the Coca-Cola Championship is like a cup final with every team out to claim our scalp. It will be a long, hard struggle to win promotion and get back to the Premiership. But we will be back eventually and we will be a stronger team if we learn the lessons of what went wrong.

FANTHOLOGY

My love of football also led me to getting involved in the business side of the game. Back in the mid-90s, as part of my academic research, I analysed the transfer market and developed a player transfer valuation system. I started to provide transfer valuations for clubs, banks and insurance companies. I got involved in the initial development of a player sale-and-leaseback scheme that allowed clubs to spread the payment of transfer fees over the whole length of the player's contract. As a Leeds fan, it was particularly pleasing to be involved in helping my own club utilise the scheme. I did the initial valuations and financial projections for the first borrowings made in the summer of 1999 that helped reinforce the squad to compete in the Premiership and the UEFA Cup. The numbers added up and I like to think that I was able to give something back to the club that I supported.

I watched the financial situation at Elland Road unfold over the next couple of years with both professional and fan interest. I had no special access to information to judge the decisions of the club's directors. I naively assumed that there was a sound business and financial strategy. I had some concerns about our continued transfer spending after failing to qualify for the Champions' League in May 2001. I wish that I had picked up on the looming financial disaster sooner. But we all have 20-20 vision with hindsight. As it was, alarm bells really started to sound in September 2002 with the publication of the financial figures for season 2001/02. A back-of-the-envelope calculation showed that the club needed to find at least £43 million to stay solvent that season. No wonder we had sold Rio Ferdinand and it was clear that there would be further player sales unless there was a change in the senior executive management and a fresh injection of cash. I was absolutely astounded by our dire financial position. I could not believe that the directors could have gambled so much on sporting success. Even though we were not in the Champions' League, we had gone out and spent £18 million on Robbie Fowler and Seth Johnson, and added another £10 million to the wage bill, all financed by borrowing £60 million against future gate receipts. It was folly of the highest order and I knew we were going to suffer big time. I strongly believe that, whatever the legal ownership of a football club, it belongs to the fans and the directors are stewards looking after a community asset.

I put my professional expertise and fan's passion to work. I made private presentations to the biggest shareholders to alert them to the financial crisis. I tried to persuade them to make changes sooner rather than later. But all to no avail. The sale of Woody forced me to go public. I made myself the financial expert on Leeds United and did countless interviews to explain the situation, why it had happened and what was needed to save our club. The club threatened legal action if I suggested that there was any danger of financial insolvency. I helped Simon Jose to form the Leeds United Independent Fans' Association (LUIFA), wrote articles for the website, handed out leaflets before home games and went to talk to supporters' groups. I came across to some Leeds fans as Mr Doom-and-Gloom and I got my share of abusive letters. But, as a fan myself, I understand the passions and I can see why I was an obvious target, particularly given the pro-board stance of some of the local media.

Boardroom changes followed and costs were cut but the playing squad bore the brunt of the economies with obvious consequences. Having just survived the relegation fight in 2002/03, it was clear that we were going to be in the relegation battle again. With no financial restructuring in sight, we were also heading to the brink of bankruptcy. The financial figures released in October 2003 confirmed what I feared. Leeds United plc was doomed and it looked as if it was going to pull down Leeds United Football Club with it. Fortunately the appointment of Trevor Birch gave us a chief executive who understood football and finance. His expertise in insolvency was much needed and we owe him a great debt of gratitude for preventing our club from going under by keeping the creditors at bay while a rescue package was negotiated.

The club was saved temporarily in March 2004 after it was taken over by Adulant Force. But the new owners had borrowed heavily to buy the club and appear to have little money to invest in it. And their 20-year season ticket scheme was repeating past mistakes of borrowing future gate receipts to cover current shortfalls. Leeds United still remains one of the most heavily indebted clubs in England. Players have been sold as a short-term fix to keep things going. Kevin Blackwell has had to put together a squad to compete in the Football League with virtually no transfer funds and a very limited wage budget. There is little prospect of the current board being successful without substantial new investment. I expect another change of ownership of our club in the near future. I will continue to offer whatever help I can to any group with the head, heart and pockets to put Leeds United back where it belongs in the top echelons of English football.

My Leeds United pedigree may not be as great as most of my fellow fans. But my passion for the club is as deep as anyone's. Leeds is my adopted home city and my daughters are Leeds born and bred. I want them to be as proud of their hometown team as much as is their dad. I want them to be able to go to Elland Road to see an exciting team committed to the badge playing in the Premiership and Europe.

We will be back. Our club, our dream, our responsibility.

Bill Gerrard

Leeds Player Names / Film Star etc Names

Pukka - part 2

Brian / Errol	FLYNN
Mark / Harrison	FORD
Arthur / Heather	GRAHAM
Eddie / Joel	GRAY
Carl / Richard	HARRIS
David / Laurence	HARVEY
Kevin / Thora	HIRD
Norman / Holly	HUNTER
Mark / Samuel L.	JACKSON
Mick / Tommy Lee	JONES
Vinnie / Shirley	JONES

RE

Where's Suffolk? Has anyone a map? It can't be that far away, can it? Kev Gaught's incredible loyalty to Leeds United includes making a round trip of 360 miles for every 'home' game.

All the way from Suffolk

I suppose my infatuation, support, love of Leeds United began on 1st May 1965 with the FA Cup Final versus Liverpool. Prior to that date, my interest in football had been high but with no real support for any professional club. Why Leeds, **180 miles** and three hours from Bury St Edmunds? Simply, one of my uncles, a staunch Red Scouser from Liverpool, suggested I watch the match at his house. Well, you had to support the opposition didn't you? 'We' lost 2-1 but, undaunted, I stuck with it. Oddly enough, that uncle's sister married a man from Leeds of all places. Of course, hearing of a new Leeds fan, he was only too keen to fuel my interest. I stayed at their house in Whitkirk several times over the years to attend matches, often during school time.

My first match was at Ipswich on 20th August 1968, with Leeds winning 3-2. I believe our first goal, scored by Mike O'Grady, was Leeds' quickest ever goal until Mark Viduka's at Charlton in March 2001. My first visit to Elland Road was on 26th August 1970 versus West Ham. 3-0 to the Whites, or Peacocks in those days. I remember standing on the huge open banking in the Lowfields Road, next to the Kop.

Attending matches over the next few years was really restricted to 'local' games; Ipswich, Norwich and games in London. Occasional visits to Elland Road were made, like the 1-0 victory over Arsenal on Monday, 26th April 1971 and the Fairs' Cup Semi Final against Liverpool two days later (thanks to a few days off school!)

On the 13th June 1974 all this was to change when I passed my driving test. Travel to matches was now no problem. The Volkswagen Beetle trooped all over the country from Manchester to Southampton to Leeds. However it wasn't until November 1980 that things really took off. An argument in a pub with an Ipswich fan - I hate them! - led to a challenge as to who would see the most matches that season. Stupid boy, by April it was no contest as I hadn't missed another match. He had.

By this time I was accompanied by my brother Popeye. Then in November 1981 we formed the East Anglia Branch of the Leeds United Supporters' Club. At its peak, around 1990, we had over 170 members. Today the number is nearer 120 but we still average about 45 at 'home' games and 20 at 'away' ones. Going by coach, compared to running our cars into the ground was sheer luxury.

In total, from the early eighties we went to see 493 consecutive matches, the run abruptly ending on 9th December 1990. Having gone to every match in the wilderness of the old Second Division, we got stuck in snow on the M6 at Rugby whilst trying to reach the biggest match of the season, Man United away. I don't think I cheered when Mel Sterland equalised!

So Everton at home on 16th December 1990 was Number One again. It was nine years before I missed another match, Wimbledon away, because my son, Lee, was playing in an important football match the same afternoon. Leeds lost 2-0 but Lee made the pass for a team mate to score the winner in the last minute, so it was worth it. Since then, I have missed only four more games, **six in total**, of every Leeds United official first team fixture since 6th December 1980.

I missed Sheffield Wednesday away when Lee played in a cup final. Leeds won 3-1, his team lost 3-1, not so good. Unless you've done it, you can't know what it feels like not to be at a match. My decision was right but that didn't stop the feeling. Lazio, away, was next. I'd been to Rome twice before to see Roma, so - same city, same ground, different colour - why bother? Being in the Champions' League, there were so many matches, I had to draw the line somewhere.

Maritimo (second time) was next. The date was 12th September 2001, yes, the day after the attack on the World Trade Center. I stepped out at Funchal airport at 10 am to be told the match had been postponed by UEFA. Why? The terrorists win again. I was less than happy when I found out that English League Cup matches were being played whilst there I was stuck on some poky island in the Atlantic Ocean. To be fair to Leeds United, they did get us home the next day and gave us a full refund but I wasn't going to pay £600 to go back the following week. We lost 1-0 and then for personal reasons I had to miss the very next match, a 2-1 win at Charlton. That's the lot, six games in twenty four years.

My 1000th match was against Chelsea in December 1997, just after Billy Bremner died. The lure of the pub meant I missed the minute's silence. Courtesy of one lad on the coach, regional television cameras descended on my house and I was featured on the local sports programme. Up to 29th August 2004, I have been to 1335 Leeds United first team matches including friendlies and testimonials.

Leeds United should be proud of their fans, the good and, to some degree, the not so good who have stuck by the club through some truly shocking periods. There has been promotion from the Second Division in 1990, then the First Division Championship in 1992, a League Cup Final in 1996 and the European matches after 2000 but that's not all that much to show for twenty four years' hard labour. On my travels, though, I have met some great characters and made some great friends; Gary 'Snake' Edwards, Coller, Mick Hewitt, Greeny, Chubby Belshaw, Cilbur, to name but a few, plus the members of our own Branch; Tim, Painy, Ray, Karen, Gerald (the coach driver) and others.

This is not written to boast or show off it's just telling how it is. When Leeds play, I go. It's almost too simple. Finally, I would like to pay tribute and dedicate this to my long suffering partner of twenty three years, Tracey, and our son, Lee. They have both put up with missing birthdays, parties, weddings, days away, etc. I love them both. We are Leeds.

Kev Gaught

Leeds Players with surnames which could be Christian names

John Charles
Arthur Graham
Johnny Giles
Gary Kelly
Jody Morris
Brian Deane
Joe Jordan
Nigel Martyn
Allan Clarke
David Harvey
Rod Wallace

MW

Fan Viewpoint - Landlord's Bitter?

'Put it this way,' says pub landlord Alwyn Hutchinson, based not far from our favourite football stadium, 'When match attendances drop by near enough 10,000 on average, you can bet local businesses and retailers suffer lower takings in similar fashion too.'

Alwyn first began supporting Leeds as a boy in the early 60's. Born and bred in rugby league-loving Featherstone ('Fev' to most Yorkshire people), it took two bus journeys to get to the stadium in those days. 'It still does, it wasn't that long ago!' he protests. Despite not being able to watch from the terraces as often as he'd like any more, his heart has remained with Leeds United and there are alternative ways of proving it if you're unable to actually attend matches. Nowadays he's in charge of Churwell's famous New Inn, high up Elland Road, and his affable manner and appearance suggest he was made to be mein host. All Leeds fans feel welcome there but the pub is possibly better known for once being under the management of a certain John Charles.

So, clearly, in view of the connection between the New Inn and King John, Leeds United's and one of the world's greatest ever footballers, Alwyn jumped at the chance of being landlord? 'No, not really, it was just an added bonus, that's all. A big bonus mind you, obviously. After all, I'm first and foremost a businessman, you can't actually live on being a Leeds fan. Unless you're very lucky.'

Such a reply makes you think certain others in the life of LUFC, perched higher on the ladder of Leeds commerce and in more privileged a position, would have benefited from chatting with Alwyn and others of his ilk.

'I think the team will be back at the top soon enough, but it won't be as quick as some folk might wish or expect,' says Alwyn. 'But I think it will do them good - let's start all over again, like we did in the sixties.'

Favourite Leeds player? 'John Giles: he was the orchestrator of so many great Leeds moves. He could kick wonderfully with either foot and his penalties were outstanding. Big Jack or Billy or Norman were always reckoned to be the hardest players in that team but I knew it was Giles, he really did bite players' legs! I liked Albert Johanneson a lot too. He was brilliant, so fast and tricky on the ball.'

Favourite goal? 'No doubt about it. Mick Jones - before busting his arm up so badly - crossed from the by-line and Allan Clarke sniffed it out and scored with a cracking diving header. Brilliant.' We don't even need to say which game he's referring to.

Favourite moment? 'A Peter Lorimer thunderbolt. He didn't score but the ball well and truly clobbered Bobby Charlton and absolutely floored him!'

Alwyn Hutchinson
Landlord, the New Inn, Elland Road, Churwell, Leeds

Chapter 3

Heroes, Gods and Humans

We want heroes, we need heroes. We have heroes.

<u>Reminiscences of a Leeds United Man</u>

Royden Wood, John Charles, Wilbur Cush, Peacock, Kerfoot, Jim Storrie, Albert Johanneson, Bobby Collins, Gary Sprake, Bremner, Charlton and Hunter. The list goes on, possibly into the hundreds. Some names are not remembered but I am sure, given the time, I could come up with many more. Their deeds though, are never forgotten.

It was about 1955 when I started supporting the team, a mere lad of nine years of age. It's as clear as yesterday. It was a cold rainy day, Everton at home, 5-1 the score, to us of course! What a start. We arrived at Elland Road, my dad, Eric Theaker, Bill Malins and others all of whom are now at that great football stadium in the sky.

I had already sat outside the pub whilst they had a pint. The atmosphere outside was magic and then it got even better. Into the ground (Lowfields Road end, as I remember it) and me to the boys' paddock. I was passed over on the shoulders of men the size of back doors, all in heavy overcoats and flat hats but everybody was so kind and so gentle, saying as they passed me down, 'Careful old love.' And then into the paddock and told to go to the front. What a great view behind that goal. After the game I waited for my dad to come and get me, climb back over the fence to join him and his team and off home to listen to Sports Report and recount the stories to the rest of the family.

HEROES, GODS AND HUMANS

Being in the catering industry and at the age of seventeen leaving home, I have not been the supporter that some people have been in attending home and away games through thick and thin, but nevertheless no matter what division they're in I am a Leeds United man.

We have seen many great moments - Raich Carter, the Revie Era, the seventies team, cup finals, league championships, games abroad, one could go on but the man who left his mark, literally, on me was the recently departed, sadly missed gentle giant: King John, John Charles.

In 1957 we played Sheffield Wednesday at Hillsborough. I wasn't very old but was very excited. We went to Sheffield by car, itself no mean feat given the standard of roads and vehicles. Hillsborough was full to bursting and, as was the way then, there was no need for stewards, only very friendly policemen. I was small in those days and the police allowed me to stand in 'the stairway' just behind the goal half way up. We were yelling like mad, we were attacking. It was raining, not a rare thing, so the ball, a real leather one with a lace, was bound to be heavy. The ball came to King John. 'Shoot!' we all shouted and he did. Boy did he hit it, straight towards the goal but just over and in to the crowd. Yes you've got it, it hit me right on the head - it didn't half hurt but boy was I proud!

I don't get chance to see them much now; as I get older I reminisce about a little incident in the Howard Wilkinson era. The board were in turmoil - nothing new there. Restructuring was in the air and it was mooted that I might be asked to become a non-executive director. What a dream. There's still time, you never know, but life has moved on. I'm still a Leeds United man and always will be. Come on Leeds!

Brian Turner, CBE

Ten of the Best Leeds Performances

10-0 Lyn Oslo (Home) Sept 1969, European Cup. Game of two halves.
3-2 Standard Liege (H) March 1970, Fairs' Cup. Came back from 2-0 down.
1-0 Manchester United (Neutral) March 1970, FA Cup Semi-Final, 2nd replay. Billy, of course, scored the winner.
2-0 Liverpool (Away) 1.1.1972, League. Happy New Year!
5-1 Manchester United, (H) Feb 1972, League. An absolute thumping.
2-1 Spurs (H) March 1972, FA Cup 6th Round. Best **ever** performance.
1-0 Arsenal (N) May 1972, FA Cup Final. Who put the ball in the Arsenal net?
2-0 Man United (A) Feb 1974, League. Total control throughout.
2-1 Barcelona (H) April 1975, European Cup Semi-Final. Against the great Cryuff.
1-0 Liverpool (H) August 1995, League. Just for Yeboah's goal.

GG

Do we sometimes expect too much from mere men?

Leeds Untied

Support for Leeds United is something that cannot be accounted for scientifically. Come to think of it, support for few clubs is to be accounted for in any rational way. As a fan, your reasoning is 'untied' from your everyday activities, which is one meaning of the title.

For many generations, dads, grandads and uncles have taken their lads, and lasses, to football matches. All that is needed is that the impressionable child goes a couple of times to a home game, and that is the beginning of a lifelong addiction. It's what happened to me as a boy, born in Bradford about half a century ago. I now live in the Netherlands, close to the beating heart of the New Europe, with Brussels, Strasbourg and Luxembourg a day trip away. Among my adopted fellow countrymen there is a genuine admiration for the Premiership in general and the type of football played by the top English clubs, in particular. And not just the Arsènes, the van Manchesteroois and the Chelseaoviches: the Dutch commercial channel, RTL 5, covers the Premiership pretty comprehensively, with many live games.

In Holland, there ARE only three clubs: Ajax, PSV and Feyenoord, and I have often been queried by football fans why I should abandon the rich pastures of the English League for the relatively barren region of the Dutch professional competition. I could easily pass myself off as a supporter of one of England's top three to win admiration, and yet, despite all these positive circumstances at the beginning of this brave new century, I am prone to the sado-masochistic ambivalence of being a Leeds United supporter.

'Perchance to dream, aye, there's the rub!'

The beginning of my own demise as a supporter lay in the mid to late sixties, when Don Revie was building a team at Elland Road on the lines of the much admired Real Madrid. The Real of di Stefano and other such immortals had dominated European football as no team had ever done before. Revie was one of those men who dared, and in large measure managed, to turn their dreams into reality.

FANTHOLOGY

There is another way in which Leeds is 'untied' rather than 'united', though. I was a student reading Classics at Leeds in the seventies. I really fell in love with the club then but couldn't help seeing the connection between what I was studying and what kept happening to Leeds. Why did they keep falling at the final hurdle? Was it their tragic flaw, what the ancient Greeks called 'hamartia'? According to the theory, in every period of true greatness in human existence, the seeds of degeneration and demise lie hidden.

There was for me in those, my formative years as a lover of the 'great game', a mightiness that only too often had its tragic side. The immortals who graced the sparkling white strip of those days: from Sprake in goal to Eddie Gray in the number 11 shirt, gave me so much to enthuse about - style, flair, courage, skill, determination and now and again (Norman, oh Norman) even sheer barbarity. You want and truly believe that total dominance for your own heroes is achievable. But even at the best of times my chosen team played its football like a Greek tragedy - bringing this team of gods, in their immaculate white, only to the very brink of dominance in English football.

I say the very brink, for somehow my gods remained all too often in second, or even third, or fourth place in the league. All too often they were the glorious, losing (semi) finalists, instead of the team that proudly held the trophy aloft. Like some latter day Achilles, it was a team often on the verge of a dominance that few other English sides have achieved, at least in domestic competition, but they had their weak heel.

There was a period of brilliance for Leeds then - just as Achilles in the war against Troy had some ten years of wonderfully good fortune, a hero warrior of the Greek army. The Leeds of Revie always had the humanity of being brilliant, yes that certainly, but also of never quite sweeping all before them. It is the tragic lot of the supporter to forget the orgasmic moments of brilliance, as when Achilles gloriously defeats Hector, prince of the Trojans, and concentrate on the arrow in the heel that saw him off. And yet my most vivid memories are the heroics of the Cup Finals against Arsenal and Chelsea, a memorable home game in the League against Southampton (result: 7-0), and suchlike feats. Sheer brilliance.

These, and many others were moments when you felt that the gods had descended from Olympus and done wonderful deeds among us. But the Leeds heroes of that era were only men. They would scale the heights, only to lose their grip just before the summit. Sniffer Clarke could sweetly meet that perfectly weighted cross from Mick Jones to score the winning goal in the Cup Final, only to fall foul of the injury to his knee, in much the same way that the local hero in my part of the world, Marco van Basten, ended far too soon his wonderful career for similar reasons. Many times I thought that Leeds just did not have that miracle ingredient, the killer instinct to take victory by the throat, to be convinced that the opposition was flawed and that they themselves could not lose. That was probably the root of their hamartia. They never quite gained the honours they deserved.

The Revie days came and finally went, followed by the doldrums of the eighties. Along came the nineties and people started noticing Leeds once more. Quality players began to gather at Elland Road, expectations began to rise again. There was a championship for Leeds, the last ever of the old First Division, under Howard Wilkinson. Then David O'Leary arrived and, before you could say 'Billy Bremner', Leeds were challengers in Europe again. We dared once more to utter such ugly profanities as 'Arsenal' and 'Manchester United' because we truly expected Leeds would take large numbers of points off them in the league.

We dared to dream again and the dream almost came true when Leeds faced Valencia in the Champions' League Semi Final. Not this time the tragic flaw of not quite believing in themselves, the team found new ways to show their human weakness and are now scattered to the four winds. The footballing gods are merciless.

'As flies to wanton boys, so are we to the gods.'

We settle down to follow the progress of our lesser heroes in the iron age of the First Division (the 'Championship') and dream of a new golden age, when this time, just maybe this time, the whites will truly earn a place in footballing history. I cannot but feel that some god somewhere is having a great joke at my expense, laughing at my naïve hopes. After all, only one of the twenty Premier teams can be champion, and three of the twenty must be relegated. But I dream that some time soon John Charles, Don Revie and Billy Bremner will look down from their mansions on high and sigh with contentment at the achievements of the club whose history they helped to form. But I'm hopeful I myself will not have to join them in those mansions first.

David Sheehan

Superleeds

Gary Sprake

Looked a Bobby Dazzler
in his light green jersey
an Adonis locks.

HEROES, GODS AND HUMANS

Lost the odd squirmer or bobbler
but sprightly Sprake took the whack
out o 'ardest shots. Flew like a flyin fox.
The boss in the box.

Paul Reaney

Cool. Collected. Calm in a crisis.
A touchline artist with a cartoon face.

Perfect. Precise. Marked as tight as his curls.
Fast on the turn. First in any foot race.

Right up probin like a surgeon. Right back
tacklin like yer life depended on im.

Kept us goin.
Got the blood flowin.

Terry Cooper

White boots. Sideboards like Stanley Baker.
Line raider. Pirate of the penalty area. Surgin
forrard, tacklin back, a liberty taker.
A real trooper. Wing Commander Cooper.

Jackie Charlton

Our Jackie.
Jackie the giraffe.

FANTHOLOGY

Lopin up for corners
he ate the grass.
Neck as long as his legs,
full head of hair flyin.
Dumped the goalie on his arse
Left forrards cryin.
A man with a mission,
to win,
then go fishin.

Norman Hunter

Consummate defender. Hunched
like a hawked avenger. Lunched
on forrards. (Liked leg meat best).

One good leg, left peg. The right
a swinger (just like his fist - good job
for wee Francis, it missed!)

Occasional sinner, but really
a bark worse than his biter.
Fair fighter.

Johnny Giles

Cultured. Confident. Soft-spoken.
Ballstroker. Playmaker. Penaltytaker.
Two fine feet. Shorts ter 'knees.
Quiet as you please. Ardest man on 'team.

HEROES, GODS AND HUMANS

Billy Bremner

Squat Jock. Brick top.
Legs as white as his kit.

Little feller. Knees like lumps
of Scottish mozzarella.

A Tartan Terror,
a real Yorkshire Terrier.

Socks rolled down,
sleeves rolled up

Sweated blood.
Elland Road muck in his veins.

Small giant. Defiant.
Lived and died for Leeds.

A legend.
A Godsend.

Peter Lorimer

Hotshot.
Took potshots
all ovver 'pitch.

Exploded
from a loaded hip.
Pocket battleship.

FANTHOLOGY

A moptop bonnie Scot.
Clean cut. Film star
looks. A blockbuster
of a right foot.

Allan Clarke

Sniffer. A poacher's nose.
Bagged chances in braces an treys.

A bandy-legged swaggerer.
Scored goals by the score.

Nineteen caps for England
an should've got more.

How shall we compare him?
Let's count the ways. Think back.

If Osgood's the Joker
An Keegan's the Queen

Clarkey's
The Ace In The Pack.

Mick Jones

Number nine.
Life on the line.

HEROES, GODS AND HUMANS

Laid it on a plate
for his team mates.

The man you'd pick first
ter stand with yer in 'trenches.
Bullet headers, shoulder charges,
put his head where it hurts.

Stoic. Heroic. Deserved
more medals than Audie Murphy.
Carried his wounds
like trophies.

Eddie Gray

Swivel hips.
Did his tricks on 'touchline.

Tantalised,
tangled an teased em
1-2-3 at a time.

Twinkle toes.
Turned on a tanner.
Left em fer dead.

On his day
better than Best,
an that's the test.

FANTHOLOGY

Paul Madeley

Upright. Elegant. All rounder.
Never a foot wrong.
Quick-witted. Wick as The Owl
on his chest. Brave as Three Lions.
Simply The Best.

David Harvey

Craggy. Caledonian. Shaggy
as a dog. Agile
as a wildcat.

Loyal as a Clansman,
he waited his chance an grabbed it -
both hands!

Superleeds poems by David Gill and Craig Bradley

Muriel, Against a Wall

Terry Cooper - 'Wing Commander' Cooper as a couple of mates of mine call him nearby - was one of the best left backs to ever pull on a shirt for Leeds United and England. Very popular was our Terry, and rightly so. But now I hate him. Seriously, I do, and you would too if you'd had similar experience of him.

It hasn't been a life-long feeling, the disliking started to show its ugly features in April 2000. I'd set out - by means of artistic creativity - to graphically remind supporters that the glories our present Leeds team seemed near to gaining probably wouldn't have existed without certain men from Leeds United past. Terry Cooper was one of those men. I wanted to paint a team 'photomural' of eighteen of the best players we've seen in the yellow, white and blue of Leeds United AFC. Born in 1965, the year Don Revie and the boys' era possibly began to rev up in earnest, I'd grown up practically worshipping Cooper and the rest of the Super Leeds gang. That is as I say, till he hurt my feelings.

There I was, in the East Stand of our hallowed Elland Road stadium during that very cold April, working my socks off to paint this mural. As the pencil and brushwork flowed, a close relationship with a wall made of breezeblock actually began to blossom. This creation was becoming my obsession. I was falling, I was, would you believe, besmitten. Finally, one chilly morning I christened her 'Muriel' and the conditions did get that little bit warmer for a while. She was my new partner and never before had I shown such commitment and dedication to a lady. Y'see, I'd recently split from my fiancée and was still hurting deeply with remorse - I'm sure most blokes know what I mean, women and football can (and do) inflict unintentional soul destroying pain - and it's hard even now to admit how weak and feeble I was and how much I allowed myself to suffer. I desperately needed a new passion, a new twinkle in my eye to take away self-harmful thoughts of my ex. In other words, I needed something to restore my sanity. Without my even realising it at first, right in front of me a divine solution was there, or more accurately, there she was.

And talking to Muriel kept me sane, though I'm well aware most people would view talking to a painting - an as yet unfinished painting at that - as being seriously deranged. Whatever, I didn't care one bit, I was on a mission and communicating with her really helped me progress. It beat listening to the same transistor radio DJs talking the same old tosh between airing the same old annoying adverts and rubbish tunes. And I swear someone was trying to torment me by playing songs my ex and I had cherished during our happier time together. Too many songs reminded me and gave me too many twinges inside. Muriel sorted me out, distracting me whenever necessary, urging me to crack on with the painting.

The cleaning and measuring of the wall, the scale drawing and even just the crouching down to etch the lower areas of the picture all made for really hard physical work. The strain on my eyes was a grind too, I sometimes felt like that cross-eyed bloke (he might've been called Ben Turpin) in those silent Hollywood comedies. And this labour of love was all unpaid and unthanked, and all during the reign of Mr Ridsdale. With him in mind you'd have thought my artwork was worthy of a few hundred quid at least wouldn't you? Per hour! Fair do's to the club, they did pay for most of the materials and granted me twenty-four hour access. By the time I'd finished though, I'd have actually preferred a twenty-four hour access denied tag, the art and graft I'd put in had just about exhausted me.

I'd taken two weeks off work to do it as well as working there three weekends on the trot. I wasn't a qualified artist (I don't really count O level Art as qualified) but muralising for Leeds United was something I'd been aspiring to do for ages. It was right up there in my ambitions of writing a novel and dating Nell McAndrew. I've done one, I'm forever hopeful of doing the other. We (the team) were doing well, we were getting capacity crowds and Elland Road was buzzing again. The quality of football O'Leary's boys were playing was often electrifying. We were becoming a major force again and it was wonderful, absolutely wonderful. The stadium manager, Harry Stokey, a likeable chap and very receptive to me doing the painting (once he'd sussed I wasn't a lunatic) gave me pretty much a free rein.

A main regret - and there are a few regards the mural - is that I didn't have time to include Mick Jones, so often the underrated star of Leeds United. He should be in the picture but, yet again, Mick Jones has been underrated as well as overlooked; and I was the guilty underrating overlooker!

Dear Mick, if you read this, I sincerely apologise, you deserve better. You were so often the unsung hero of Super Leeds (though not alone in that respect) and I still always wince when you busted your arm helping us win the Cup in '72. (I tell you what though, if I'd been you I'd have insisted the Queen came down to the Wembley pitch to give me my medal). She did look really worried though, it has to be said.

I hereby apologise to you too Gary Edwards, I saw you on Look North once saying that Jonesy was your favourite all time player. I meant no harm.

One of my favourites was Duncan McKenzie (*For he's the king of foo-ootball!*) as well as marauding left back Tony Dorigo. They're not in the mural either and I'm pretty ashamed of that as well. And don't get me on about which managers I should have included, that would have trebled the time taken just agonising over whether Messrs Graham, O'Leary and Wilkinson deserved to be in the same picture as Don Revie. Looking back, none of it could have happened without Don Revie so he should also be in the painting as lone Manager.

For nigh on nearly twenty solid cold days, I'd trudge down Wesley Street with a bucket and heavy holdall of materials dragging on my shoulder early each morning. I had to work frequently in dim light and sub-zero temperatures with nothing but four layers of clothing and stale butties for dinner to keep me warm. Cups of piping hot tea, as promised by one of the security guys, never materialised. To be fair, it's a longer walk from their office around to the East Stand than you might think and he had 'proper' work to do no doubt. Later, around 6 p.m. each day, squinting and just about done in, back I'd struggle up that swine of a hill, weighed down even more by the holdall and co. I was close to passing out by the time I reached the top of the hill, no exaggeration.

I can't categorically state it as fact for every other 'painter' in the land but for my part it's true: I fell in love with colour. Not red obviously, that would be unnatural, but certainly with yellow, white and blue, the predominant colours of the Leeds squad painting. With all the pleasure, preparation and care put in to a painting project, it's bound to happen. The devotion and time spent just mixing the paints, staring at the rich, beautiful blends I'm creating as I stir, stir, stir, causes a sensation of all embracing fondness, dedication and loyalty flooding my thoughts. Transfixed by the wonderful colours I was making, I frequently drifted to another, happier world.

A sad aspect of the matter - for me at least - is that the 'Eighteen of the Best' painting is not particularly that good. It would have been much better if I'd been able to afford more time and if some form of heating had been provided. In fact, if someone had bothered to just check to see that I hadn't actually died from hypothermia, that would have been a pleasant bonus. At least I wasn't working alone; not only did I have Muriel to listen to me but the players often demanded my undivided attention too. The studious work on their portraits provided a strange and private rapport with each one - except Terry Cooper - and I had to concentrate on each face almost as if I was interrogating them. In my darker personal moments I suffered real confidence crises with regard to my abilities, struggling to get good likenesses with certain faces, telling myself I was failing badly and making a real fool of myself. I even got the physical shakes more often than I care to remember. In really desperate times I even heard myself demanding 'What the hell have you got yourself in to?!'. But sense prevailed - reminders that the worst thing that could happen here would be for me to quit and whitewash over the painting, feeling at the same time a very deep but temporary red-faced shame. 'Red' again, it's just not nice. Like a relegation, I would get over it in time and bounce back.

I was confident I'd get the actual Leeds colours right and the various kit designs authentic enough, but could I chuff convince myself I was getting a good likeness in all of the players. Lucas Radebe for instance. You'd think he'd be one of the easiest faces to portray. I mean, let's be honest, you only need to draw the widest and lovely white smile and the unique haircut to get him accurate, was I wrong? No, I wasn't. It wasn't the skin tone that was the problem either - that was a cracking shade of brown, easily made - it was the bewildering impression I was getting that, the more I painted him, the more he was resembling another person. And not just any old person either but one who owned the same initials. Seriously, our LR, my Lucas Radebe, at times uncannily looked like Lionel blooming Richie!

Dr Radebe and Mr Richie might make a decent book title. Well, maybe not.

Any road, never mind 'Hello' and 'Dancing on the Ceiling', I was seriously thinking of a very hasty goodbye and hurtling down the stairway. Hurling down the stairway even, if I wasn't careful I'd be worrying myself sick with it.

I pulled myself together and eventually managed to make a good likeness of Lucas, I think. I often wonder if he ever listens to The Commodores though, or Lionel's later solo material. And did Lionel ever fancy watching the lads play at Elland Road, he'd be more than welcome?

Some of the other weaknesses in the painting are not all of my own making, it has to be noted. And I realised that a Roy of the Rovers comic book style would be my best chance of success even though I'd entered the venture with the hope of creating fantastic lifelike portraits. It had soon become clear I was no where near talented enough to achieve such quality and I had too little time anyway. I'm not putting myself down, it's a simple fact, that's all. For instance, could I ummers get decent photos to work from of Harry Kewell, John Charles, Nigel Martyn and the devil that was Terry Cooper. Fair enough, I had reasonable enough if not ideal photos of Charlesy and 'Village' Martyn to refer to but Kewell and Cooper, they were nightmares. I drew Kewell from a passport size photo. The result isn't such a bad job, except alas Terry Cooper's portrait; he looks more like Henry Cooper to me, even Tommy Cooper. Or even Jilly Cooper. He was the last face I finished - yes, it is finished to any critics out there - and I wish I'd replaced him with Dorigo.

This is how Muriel, my Eighteen of the Best Leeds United Through the Ages squad lines up.

Nigel Martyn - with shoulders wider than Briggate in the picture, we should never have let him leave, he was that good even at 37. The number of saves he made with seemingly no earthly right to do so was immense and he's the main reason we didn't get relegated early in his Leeds career. We've actually never done badly for goalies at Leeds but they usually get remembered for the clangers they drop, notably Sprake and Lukic. They, together with Harvey, Day, Robinson and Sullivan, have at times been fantastic for us.

Paul Reaney - with a questionable skin tone here but in life his speed and talent was never in question. I might have let him down with the picture quality but he never let the Leeds fans down. His pace, as far as I remember, was phenomenal and he loved marauding down that right flank. I'd be hard pushed to name a better right back ever since, too.

Terry Cooper - enough said already (his picture contains really nice white boots though), he was still one of the best attacking full backs to play in the British game. Imagine playing against him on the left and Reaney on the right, as attacking defenders, you'd want to pack the game in!

Billy Bremner - his hair's a bit too orange but his exceedingly pale skin is accurate and there's no mistaking it's Billy, probably the archetypal face of Leeds United ever to have appeared. On the pitch he was everywhere and he was the epitome of what a team captain should be, leading, compelling his players, never giving up and never letting others let the side down. Look in the dictionary under 'spirit' or 'passion' and it should read Billy Bremner.

Bobby Collins - with wonky legs in the painting (something that he often inflicted on opponents in real life, allegedly) he was one of the main reasons Revie's team made it in the first place. You'd have Bobby in the trenches with you for sure. I always wondered how much influence he had on Billy Bremner, that never say die, never stop fighting spirit. I warrant without Bobby Collins there would have been a lesser Billy Bremner. My Dad claims I'm called

Robert after Bobby Collins but my Mum won't have it, saying it's after Robert the Bruce!

David Batty - a good likeness, though with him smiling and not actually snarling! It was obvious he learned lessons from Bremner though Batts never scored - or even tried to - enough goals. Renowned or notorious depending on which team you supported, for his hard tackling and shin-nipping, he should have been recognised for his excellent passing ability too. Shouldn't have took that penalty though!

Jack Charlton - surprisingly just about the easiest for me to recreate. I put '66' on his shorts too, as he was our one true World Cup hero (besides Les Cocker in the England backroom team though some might say that doesn't count). What an inspiration Jack was, on and off the field in my opinion, and a great tackler and especially header of the ball.

Norman Hunter - complete with trendy flowing locks but I bet no one took the micky, he'd have had them for mincemeat! I wasn't aware whether he was as good as Bobby Moore but there were those that said he was. I bet at least he was quicker. He was another player famous or infamous for his hard tackling and 'leg biting' but he had a sweet left peg too did Norman. I seem to remember he scored the winner once with a belter from outside the area - against Leeds, as player manager of Bristol City. I bet he keeps quiet about that; he should do!

Paul Madeley - Leeds' real Rolls Royce - I might be biased as he went to Cross Flatts Park Middle School where I went later - and as with the classic car, never used enough for England and treated like a luxury. I had a few problems for a while getting a good likeness of him but I think I finally made it. There wasn't much he couldn't do and he was fast as fury, though 'fury' is never a word you'd truly associate with Madeley as he was a true gentleman and sportsman of football

Lucas Radebe - we've been blessed with some class central defenders over the years, haven't we?! Lucas is right up there in the list of Unlucky With Injuries too though, unfortunately. His smile is a dazzler and his pace and tackling was like lightning. Another world title winner too while at Leeds: FIFA's Fair Play Player of the Year, not a bad little accolade that, and richly deserved, ask any Leeds or South Africa fan.

Peter Lorimer - golden boots Lash Lorimer, what a player, what a striker of the pig's bladder and what a blooming hard time I had drawing him! The finished portrait was worth the strife though and I'm very glad he's still associated with the club at a time when sticking by those you care for really matters. The Scottish FA deserve severe grief for the pitiful number of times he was allowed to play for Scotland. You think Beckham and Gerrard can strike a ball well? They're not worthy of mention in the same breath.

Gordon Strachan - hair maybe too orange again and yet another Scottish midfield general with that crucial never give in belief. In my opinion he had similar effect on Leeds to that of Bobby Collins' in the early '60's. Strachan was a real dynamo and it's no coincidence we won promotion and the League with him in charge of the midfield.

John Giles - under-appreciated I think, he was still regarded as one of the world's best passers of the ball. Difficult to paint though, more so than Lorimer in fact and I'll tell you a secret: painting Johnny was very painful for me, because his eyes are just like my ex's, no word of a lie. And no, I'm not saying I ever fancied Gilesy, just that their eyes were similar, frighteningly so.

We bought him off Man U, I'm not sure everyone knows that (and Strachan). Eric Cantona would never have made it in to this line up even if we hadn't sold him, I'm sure of it.

Tony Currie - always looked immaculate in the yellow Admiral kit; though the likeness isn't great here you know it's him straight away (I hope). Yet another great mercurial England player who played too few games for the national team, to their shame. Always better than Hoddle, too, though both used to hit fantastic fifty, sixty yard passes right on to the toe of team mates.

Eddie Gray - just about everyone's favourite over the eras of Leeds. His hair's painted a bit too long and dark I think, like Norman's. He had as bad luck as Lucas with injuries. Many supporters won't have seen him play and pale coloured videos don't really do him justice, which is a shame but such is life. He was that good, that's all you need to know!

Harry Kewell - an impostor? Maybe, or maybe a bit of a harsh accusation; I sometimes do wish I hadn't bothered though, especially as he looks like a cartoon character in the painting. His skill was unquestionable but his attitude wouldn't have got him in to Melchester Rovers' team even, he sometimes looked like he couldn't be bothered. All that talent but with apparently little passion or determination, he might better be likened to the so-laid-back-he's-near-horizontal Pink Panther!

Allan Clarke - his hair colour was hard to get right - so I didn't bother! - but there was only one Sniffer, unmistakeable I'd say. More recent football fans would tell you Ian Rush or Robbie Fowler were brilliant finishers - and they're right obviously (not that we really witnessed it for Leeds) - but Clarke was just as lethal and a better all round player

John Charles - 'King John' all I really had was an old black and white photo to work from so I admit it's not a brilliant effort, but I tried my hardest and that's all I think truly matters. You know who it is and he definitely stands out, just like his lifetime. I met him a couple of times and he was as pleasant as people would have you believe, a lovely, modest fella. His skill as a player was legendary, his warmth as a man no myth

NB - nods also of acknowledgement to Tony Yeboah, Lee Chapman, Mel Sterland, Mark Viduka, David Harvey, Woodgate, Trevor Cherry, John Sheridan, Andy Ritchie, Ian Baird, Mervyn Day, Chris Whyte, Gary McAllister, Dominic Matteo and any players influential enough in the future to get us back in to the top division.

Lots of people have commented on Muriel; I've heard her described as 'rubbish' right through to the top of the table as 'fantastic'. Being completely honest, I think it's neither, it's 'okay', simple as that. Don't get me wrong, I am proud of it and I'm actually grateful to the painting because it allowed me to get rid of a lot negative crap from my life, strange as that may sound. Any form of art making is cathartic, I'm sure of it, it does the soul and the spirit genuine good, just like in fact, sport, especially football. By the time I got down to my muralising I really had let myself become poorly with worry and stress. But the more I drew and painted the more I felt my spirits and my lust for life slowly growing, even though the work was a real slog.

YOU might hate it, you might love it; but as Leeds United fans I know you'll have opinions on it. You may even feel urge to add to it or indeed detract from it, who knows? I'll tell you something for sure though: within that mural is much of my heart and soul, I mean it. There's no need for me to apologise for exaggerating because I'm not exaggerating, I'm telling the truth, believe me.

In the end, those qualities - heart and soul - are the least I want to see from Leeds United players.

A player not committing their Self to the cause of Leeds United is, in my eyes, unforgivable. Leeds United fans, players, officials, all should be For the mutual cause, nothing else. Why bother doing anything if you're not prepared to give it your all?

Robert Endeacott

Player Names Ending in 'a'

Masinga
McKenna
Agana
Cantona
Camara
Kamara
Sabella
Viduka
Lorima
Hunta
Bremna
Coopa

Autograph hunter

Football has changed a lot since I was a lad. And I'm only 23. *Footballers* have changed a lot from when I was a lad, too. My uncle took me to my very first Leeds match, our 4-1 Boxing Day triumph over Chelsea, back in 1990 and in the few years since then, key aspects of the game have changed beyond almost all recognition. In brief, too much money has altered the culture of English football and footballers have lost touch with the fans, the people who, in the end, pay their wages.

After the death of John Charles, the Yorkshire Evening Post published a picture of the Leeds legend in his prime - leaning over the fence of his corporation house chatting to a group of short-trousered young Leeds United fans, enthralled by meeting their hero. I cut it out and kept it. A truly special image of a truly special player and man. But how strange - how alien - that image now seems in our days of footballers sitting in country mansions fronted by imposing metal gates, their young fans only able to secure an autograph on the player's 'home turf' if they manage to catch him in a co-operative mood, as his film-star standard car sweeps towards or from his film-star standard house. But then of course there is the club shop signing - where the football stars' autographs can be bought for the cost of outrageously priced items of clothing. It was easy to have access to John Charles for a handshake and autograph when he was on the tram trundling to Elland Road on match days. It is a much stiffer task for today's youngsters to obtain the autograph of the latest one-season wonder when he speeds his way to and from a football ground in his deluxe sports car (price: one week's wages).

Like many fans, I was once a young autograph hunter. Most of the Leeds players I was lucky enough to meet were willing to sign my copy of Don Warters' 1979 hardback, *Leeds United: The Official Club History*. In its inside-cover the scribbled signatures of Leeds players from different eras jostled with each other for space. If I ran into a Leeds player by chance - meaning I didn't have my book to hand - I would take the scrap of paper, envelope or whatever they had emblazoned their signature upon and carefully tuck it into my book for safekeeping, where their signature would join the ranks of all-time greats (and all-time not-so-greats).

My *Official Club History* inside-cover 'team' included Lee Chapman, Eric Cantona, Paul Reaney, Bobby Collins, Tony Yeboah, Dylan Kerr, Gary McAllister, David Batty and Gordon Strachan amongst many others. I salivated at the thought of various members of my inside-cover 'team' on the football pitch - at the same time. Together on the pitch just as they were together on the page. At their peak. I imagined Yeboah and Cantona teaming up as Leeds United strikers. I conjured up images of Bobby Collins and Gordon Strachan running the Leeds midfield together. I'd have been delighted to get Norman Hunter to sign my book alongside David Batty's signature. I could then have imagined Hunter and Batty knocking the hell out of a visiting Manchester United team, under the laxer refereeing rules of Hunter's days, of course.

Filling, and trying to fill, the inside-cover of that book sheds light on just how much football and *footballers* have changed since I first started adding to it with celebrity scribble at the age of 10 or 11. It would be impossible now to collect autographs the way I used to. The first autograph I got was that of David Batty. This was a prize one to obtain because we viewed Batty as symbolic of all that was best about Leeds United - tough, committed, uncompromising, unpopular with rival teams. Most importantly, Batty was a local lad in our local team.

We had found out on the neighbourhood 'grapevine' that Batty lived in a house just off Shadwell Lane, not ten minutes walk from my own North Leeds home. Numerous local boys had gone there for Batty's signature. As soon as I found out the news, I was desperately eager to capitalise on it and start off my Leeds United autograph collection. The next day, I was ready to walk the ten minutes to my idol's house. I was so excited about the opportunity to get his signature - and perhaps even actually meet him - that I felt I must go straight away. But since Leeds were playing at Old Trafford later that day surely I had missed my chance until tomorrow at the earliest? Yet to my eleven-year old, Leeds United-obsessed mind the solution was clear: go early in the morning. Very early in the morning.

My calculations of players' match day arrangements for an away game in Manchester led me to the conclusion that if I knocked on Batty's door at 8.30 a.m. I would be sure to find him in. And indeed he was in. I nervously knocked and his wife Mandy answered. I explained the situation. Given the time it was, perhaps she was disappointed that it wasn't the postman with a parcel but was instead a nervous young Leeds United fan. But Mandy smiled - despite the early hour - and explained that 'David' (my friends and I just knew him as 'Batty'!) was still in bed. However, she said that it was no problem at all and if I told her my name she would get him to sign something for me. I duly informed her and minutes later she came back with a photo of Batty ('David') in action, taken in the 1990-91 season. As to be expected, it was of him looking customarily fearsome in his midfield role. He had written "To Richard, Best Wishes, David Batty". To use the football cliché, I was absolutely over the moon, David (and Mandy).

I marched home with my new, prize possession, anxiously guarding it in case some wind or rain of ill fortune conspired to smudge the blue ink. The signed photograph did not go straight into my *Official Club History*, I blue-tacked it onto my wall. From then on this 11-year old felt a personal bond with 'David' and I felt sure that my crack-of-dawn visit to his home had inspired Batty to help Leeds secure a 1-1 away draw with Manchester United later that day. Surely the memory of this example of the unbridled commitment of a local young fan had spurred him on to help achieve an excellent result against our most hated rivals? A year or so later, Batty had moved up in the world and out of that house. He had apparently gone to somewhere in or around Wetherby.

The legendary Bobby Collins could be found on my street. My star-struck youthful memories of him were that he was a man who chatted to my mum and dad about repairs to his car - both our families had a Fiat. He, also, was very happy to oblige when as a young lad I knocked on his door and asked for an autograph. His signature was doubly prized because it had the feeling of a gem from times of old - and it impressed older relations incredibly. Bobby worked as a driver for Leeds City Council after retiring from being one of the best footballers of his - or indeed any - generation. Most of the current football 'stars' wouldn't be fit to lace his boots.

A wonderful memory which stays with me is from the 1992/93 season - at the traffic lights near the Casino at Moortown Corner in North Leeds. I was in the car on the way to church with my mum and she stopped as the lights went red. Glancing around I noticed a familiar face in the car next to ours, that of England and Leeds midfielder David Rocastle. He saw the delighted expression of sudden recognition on my face and gave a broad grin back and stuck his thumb up as the lights turned to green and both cars drove off. This memory of a jovial David Rocastle made me even more sorry a few years later when I heard the tragic news of his death at the age of just 33.

The last 'journey' of my career as a youthful autograph-hunter came during the Yeboah-craze. During the time that some of us warped the pronunciation of his name so that we could sing "Oooooh, aaaaaaaah, Ye-bo-aaaah" as part of our attempts to exorcise the pain of the departure of our darling French striker in the 1992/93 season. Ever-alert surveillance from young fans in the area provided the intelligence that Yeboah lived just off Wigton Lane in Alwoodley. Another address just ten minutes from that of my own. So I set off, intent on getting Yeboah to sign both my *Official Club History* and my new trainers.

He wasn't in. But his wife was. She saw me standing there in my Leeds United shirt with 'Yeboah' on the back with a number 9 rather than his actual squad number of 23 - a symbol of my passionate (and quite correct) belief in the vast superiority of Yeboah to the then de-facto holder of the prized number 9 shirt, Brian Deane. Mrs. Yeboah informed me that 'Tony' wasn't in and I thought my chance had gone. But then she kindly volunteered the information that he would be back in three quarters of an hour and if I would like to come back then he would be happy to meet me and I could get his autograph. I was very impressed - this was someone being much more kind and helpful than they needed to be.

Three quarters of an hour later I returned and Mrs. Yeboah showed me in to the living room where Tony Yeboah was sitting. He invited me to sit down. He chatted to me about which position I played and then signed my trainers, asking if they were new and saying what nice trainers he thought they were. I thought this was particularly kind of him to say to a youngster - he was used to eager potential sponsors giving him the most expensive football boots around and my trainers, though I liked them and though they were a decent make, were not particularly expensive or flashy.

As I walked up the street away from the Yeboah household, I saw his delightful young daughter playing on a little bike. She asked me, 'Have you just been to see my dad?' I, still excited, said, 'Yes - your dad is the best player.' The little girl paused and then replied, 'No, he's not that good,' before bidding me a cheerful farewell. The last journey in the travels of this youthful autograph hunter was his best ever.

It is as well that I have shelved my *Official Club History* and no longer seek to fill its inside-cover with the signatures of Leeds United stars, because it is very rare now for me to see footballers. The huge increase in wealth has driven them from the 'posh' North Leeds to the even posher 'golden triangle' of Wetherby, Linton and Boston Spa, much less in touch with ordinary fans.

I have come across players though, but in less happy circumstances and it is almost as if my leaving childhood and the loss of innocence is mirrored by how and where I have since encountered my 'heroes'. As a young Saturday night drinker out in Leeds city centre, I have occasionally seen footballers out and about. I remember seeing Lee Sharpe jump out of a taxi by the Majestyk night club opposite The Queen's Hotel in City Square, dumping an empty beer bottle on a metal roadside railing. Leeds had been defeated away at Tottenham merely hours earlier. I remember thinking that, from the look of his jaunty gait and the fact that he couldn't wait until he actually got to the nightclub to have a drink, he seemed to have forgotten all about how Leeds had turned in a dreadful performance and dropped 3 points. He just seemed anxious to be out on the town. As a Leeds fan, I for one was mightily hacked off we had been such an easy pushover for Tottenham.

One Saturday night, during the David O'Leary era, I saw a Ben Sherman-shirted Lee Bowyer swaggering through the town centre with a group of lads, looking every inch like the kind of aggressive young male you avoided making eye contact with when out drinking. Funny that. I hear tell, too, of how a left-footed

Australian, no longer with Leeds, was too busy to receive the Handicapped Supporters' Player of the Year award. Unthinkable once.

Instead of dwelling on these later memories, however, I choose to focus on those like David Batty's uncomplaining compliance at 8.30 a.m. on the morning of an away match or the hospitality of Tony Yeboah and his family; or those of the cheerful all-time-great Bobby Collins; and on David Rocastle's happy grin and raised thumb at the traffic lights. And I like to look at that picture which seems to symbolise all of these wonderful occasions: John Charles leaning over the fence of his corporation house, chatting to a group of delighted short-trousered young Leeds United fans. Lower wages might just bring the players back to us again.

Richard Burgon

Leeds Player Names / Film Star etc Names

PUKKA - part 3

Seth / Celia	JOHNSON
Joe / Louis	JORDAN
Gary / Grace	KELLY
Dylan / Deborah	KERR
Aaron / John	LENNON
Gordon / Steve	McQUEEN
Danny / John	MILLS
David / Michael	RENNIE
Frazer / Ralph	RICHARDSON
David / Cliff	ROBERTSON
Paul / Edward G.	ROBINSON

FANTHOLOGY

Profile of a Leeds fan - Louise Rennison

She might be a best-selling writer of teenage fiction in both Britain and America but as soon as 'our brave lads' are mentioned, Leeds-born Louise Rennison is just a United fan, like the rest of us. The wacky heroine of her stories is, she happily admits, based on her own teens. She has her heroes, too, a whole host of them - the entire Leeds team of Don Revie's era.

In fact the idea of heroes is a recurring theme as she talks with undimmed enthusiasm about the club she has supported all her life, whilst acknowledging the many disappointments fans have had to put up with since the Glory, Glory days. She is convinced that current Leeds fans both want and deserve heroes. When she, herself, feels down it is to football videos of those days that she often returns for inspiration.

'We want people with the right spirit playing for Leeds. I can take failure as long as it's heroic failure,' she says, going on to elaborate. 'Flogging your guts out. That's a real Yorkshire trait. Scrapping for Leeds.' Grit and determination are, to her, the best qualities. Epitomising the county and the city's character, they have shaped the club's approach to the game throughout its history. 'When anyone signed for Don Revie's team, Leeds changed the way they played rather than them changing the way Leeds played.' It is clear that is how she thinks it still should be because it is a central part of our club's tradition. For Louise, Jackie Charlton sums up that spirit perfectly, especially when contrasted with brother Bobby. Bobby was undoubtedly more skilful: Jack undoubtedly had much more character, even if he was always liable to wander off up field and needed Norman to keep a constant eye on him. He always played with passion and commitment.

She herself has displayed the same characteristics, having carved out a successful career as an entertainer, writer and broadcaster, and is very conscious of how the city of Leeds formed her personality. She is honest, opinionated and forthright in an engaging way that people from the north understand so well.

Allied to team spirit, is leadership. Good captaincy, especially with that Scots' fire encapsulated by Billy Bremner, she sees as vital. 'The bond between captain and players is crucial to a successful team. It's like in the film "Master and Commander". The chain of command is there but works best because they are a unit. You need leadership but you also need the right response to it. Each player has a connection with the team as a whole.' We discuss the less than total commitment of some fairly recent players before the subject is tactfully dropped.

She went to her first game at Elland Road as a twelve-year old back in the early sixties, along with her dad and her friend Sheila. She vividly remembers, however, that her dad insisted on them learning all the playing positions, like right half and inside left, on the morning of the match before he would agree to take them. Being a keen hockey player actually made it quite easy since both games used the same formation but the rule had been set; understand the game so you can appreciate it more. Soon Louise, Sheila and a group of other girls were making the regular trip to home matches. She remembers with affection the mounting excitement as the bus neared the stadium. Then the quickening walk, 'Until, eventually, you lost your individual identity, being gradually absorbed into the converging crowd.'

A burgeoning career took her to London in the seventies and she is Brighton-based these days, but she has always remained loyal, attending matches when she can, particularly on her regular trips to Leeds. In a way, it has been a means of keeping in touch with her own roots. She toured for four years with a one-woman, autobiographical show called "Stevie Wonder Felt My Face". In one part of it, she tells of the wonderful childhood memory when she rang Billy Bremner and actually spoke with him. Proudly, she talks of how, when touring Scotland, the Glasgow Herald asked her to write a feature about her hero, based on that event.

It must be incredible for any young supporter nowadays, in an age when players fancy themselves as film stars demanding total privacy, to know that the young Louise was able to telephone and then speak to her idol by simply looking up his name and number in the phone book. The thrill of talking to Billy Bremner was and still is really important to her because, for all the sense of being absorbed into the crowd, she also believes we need an individual relationship with the club and its players. We each feel something personal about our support for Leeds United.

Part of that can be because of how our support for Leeds fits in with our family relationships. This was true for Louise and her dad. 'As a girl, I used to go to football matches with him. When I was a teenager, we couldn't talk about anything else but could still talk about football. It became this big metaphor for other things we were trying to say.'

This link between her family and Leeds was movingly captured on John Peel's radio show Home Truths when she read her account of how, after she had broken up with a boyfriend, her dad took her down to Elland Road to watch United training. It was his way of trying to help her overcome her sadness. Before Thorp

Future Leeds legend greets present Leeds legend.

'King' John talking to some of his young South Leeds subjects.

1971, Fairs Cup victors over Juventus.

1972, at last!

1974 - the Title-holding gods wave to the Kop faithful.

Champions! 1974, Billy & Don at captain Bremner's testimonial.

Yet another unprovoked attack on Leeds fans by the constabulary.

Leeds v QPR, 1987 - note the fantastic four floodlights!

Some memorable
Leeds match
programmes.

Wembley 1996, the only fireworks Leeds fans see all day!

Above: European fun nights, part 1 - Italy.

Below: European fun nights, part 2 - Spain.

Oystein's Family Album (Boden 2004)

Hampshire LU Supporters' Club - a barbecue.

'Marching On Together', forever.

May 2004

Arch, players used to practise on pitches near the West Stand. Unfortunately, training had finished but they managed to persuade a groundsman to let them on to the actual pitch. Once through the players' tunnel and on to the hallowed turf, her father gave a commentary as they mimed an attacking movement with an imaginary ball. 'Rennison passes to Rennison and quickly moves for the return.' So the commentary continued until Louise scored with a shot into the unprotected goal. Surely every fan's dream come true?

She has clear views on how important the club's fans are and also on how strong the bond should be between players and supporters. 'There has to be a connection between the fans and the team. Not only that but each fan needs to feel special. There is something exclusive about each fan's relationship.' She feels this is because such a strong emotional response is inspired in the fans. 'When I was older I was in love with all the players. Not in a real sense so that wives or girlfriends might feel threatened but I was still each player's girlfriend.' When the idea was put to her that she might feel like an Earth mother to them, she replied, 'No, but an Earth girlfriend, yes.'

She is, by disposition, an optimist and sees good times ahead for her beloved club. 'Leeds is such an attractive place and such a resilient one, too. We will bounce back.' One of the indirect advantages of having gone into financial meltdown is that the slate has been wiped clean in more ways than one. 'It's like we are starting from scratch. Football, by its nature, is youthful and hopeful. We have a great future but we must have the right principles and philosophy. The supporters are part of the team, part of a large family and it is those familiar virtues of courage and fairness that we need.'

FANTHOLOGY

Louise Rennison feels and talks passionately about Leeds United. Her dream for the future possibly goes into overdrive at times but that's what being a fan can do to you, once you start talking about your heroes.

GG

Leeds Player Names / Film Star etc Names

PUKKA - part 4

Ian / Geoffrey	RUSH
John / Robert	SHAW
Alan / Will	SMITH
David / James	STEWART
Bob / Elizabeth	TAYLOR
Gwyn / Terry	THOMAS
Chris / Kathleen	TURNER
Andy / Emily	WATSON
Jason / Paula	WILCOX
Gary / Robin	WILLIAMS

Chapter 4

A Tour of the Worldwide Whites

Over the years Leeds United has developed a global fan base. The following contributors show remarkable loyalty and affection for the club and it is particularly striking what efforts fans make to watch their beloved team.

<u>Copenhagen</u>

I have been a Leeds fan for about thirty years, my oldest memory being of me doing my homework in front of the tv and watching United lose to Bayern Munich in 1975.

I do not know why I love Leeds. It feels right and that's just the way it's always been. Perhaps it is because Leeds were really great in the '70's and probably one of the teams shown regularly on tv in Denmark back then.

When I left school at seventeen, I decided to go to England and work as an au pair. The perfect first choice was, of course, to find a family in Leeds. I lived with a wonderful family in Leeds for fourteen months and never missed a home game during that period. Those were the days - and Leeds have been in my heart and on my mind ever since.

After returning home it was hard to keep up with the news from Elland Road and when playing in the Second Division it was impossible, as apparently no one is interested in Second Division football! Fortunately, today, I can find news and information whenever I please, thanks to the internet and the 'short distances' we have now.

I have been to London a couple of times to watch Leeds play, I went to Varberg in Sweden in 2000 and visited Elland Road again for the first time in twenty five years on 25th April 2004, to see us beaten by Portsmouth. That was a massive and emotional experience despite defeat and near certain relegation. I promised myself that I wouldn't wait that long until my next visit, which I hope I can keep!

The entrance to my flat is a homage to Leeds United. Decorated with wallpaper, scarves, caps, pictures and a giant jigsaw puzzle I bought in Leeds in 1977. Once a Leeds United fan, always a Leeds United fan.

Leeds forever

Annette Tandrup, Denmark

I didn't choose them, they chose me.

Since I started to follow football, English football has always been the one for me, naturally alongside that of my native Finland, but before I arrived in England, I didn't have a favourite team, I just watched all matches on tv.

I first came to England in 1998, to work here for a year in Wakefield. Naturally, in 'God's Own County' life was just Leeds, Leeds and Leeds. Finally one day I had a chance to go to Elland Road. I heard from the radio that the next day United were playing an FA Cup replay at home and, because I had a day off, I rushed in to the Leeds Club shop in the Wakefield Ridings Centre to buy myself a ticket.

A TOUR OF THE WORLDWIDE WHITES

The match was 13th January 1999 against Rushden and Diamonds. My seat was on the Upper Tier of the East Stand and I remember the moment I stepped in and saw the green turf under the floodlights, it was a more impressive sight than any stadium before, and I had been in a few, including Wembley. And when I heard 'Marching on Together' for the first time - I got goosebumps! I had not chosen Leeds, they had chosen me, on that chilly night in January.

In the match day programme I saw an advertisement for a half season ticket and with all the money I had in my account, borrowing some from my friend and my boss and begging my mum to send me some from home, I managed to get enough to buy a ticket for the West Stand. That spring was the best in my life. I still remember the sight of thousands of white shirts under the blue Yorkshire sky, and I still believe it never rains in Yorkshire, when Hasselbaink scored against Man U.

After a year spent back in the old country I moved to study in Preston, and learned how it feels to be the only Leeds fan around and being mocked by everyone else. Still, I made my pilgrimage to Elland Road as often as I could, but mainly I went to away games. For a poor student it was much cheaper and easier to get to places like Liverpool, especially because getting from Leeds back to Preston after a midweek game was a nightmare. Luckily the local pubs, bless 'em, were there with their giant screens with the odd LUFC match showing.

Especially towards the end of my studies, Leeds' financial problems had come up, and it took a lot of courage to go to football training with my Leeds top, because everyone else was supporting Liverpool or Man U. All this was piece of cake compared to what was to come...

Now I find myself in Manchester because I can't find a job in Yorkshire. Leeds' fortunes have gone down and all I see around me are these Japanese tourists thinking they look cool and dapper in their Man U shirts. I see many Irish Man U season ticket holders in my work (not all Man U fans come from London, apparently!) and try, sadly unsuccessfully, to convince them to change their allegiance.

Despite living in enemy territory, I am not hiding my true colours and some might even call my actions suicidal. Or what do you think? It is a Saturday in May 2004. Man City are at home against Newcastle and Leeds are playing next day at Bolton. Leeds, as we know, needed to win and we needed Man City to lose. What do I do? Yes, what DO I do? I'm roller skating to work, and as it happens, my route goes past the City of Manchester Stadium. It is around 1.30 in the afternoon so the stadium is buzzing and there am I, in my Leeds top, skating through the blue half of Manchester. 'Going down, going down, going down' is ringing in my ears from every corner, coupled with a few 'Oi, Dingle, where's yer sheep?' questions. Crazy? Yes, I might be.

'LUFC to Div.1' is scribbled on the dusty van near where I take a bus to work. Yes, it might be a message for me. I don't care. I hold my head up high, kiss the badge on my replica top and go on. I'm Leeds and I'm proud of it!

Piia Suomalainen, Finnish exile

Double Dublin

1) Why Leeds?

Why Leeds? To be honest that's a question I just don't know the answer to. As the sole Leeds supporter in my family (sole football supporter full stop, actually) the reason why I chose to support this club, even though it is steeped in history, is completely beyond me. Asked why I support Leeds, no one EVER believes that it's not because my dad or my brother supported them, no matter how many times I tell them no one else in my family does. What I do know is that I definitely made the right choice. There's 91 other clubs in England I could've chosen, not to mention the Irish League clubs, but there isn't one of those clubs I'd rather support.

The past two years as things grew worse and worse and it felt like my heart had been ripped out and torn into tiny little pieces, I never once thought I should support someone else. Admittedly there have been times when I've wanted to stop caring but I just couldn't. No matter how bad things get there's always still that tiny little bit of optimism that always bursts through and tells me that everything will be alright.

Maybe there is no reason for choosing Leeds. Maybe it's simply because as the song goes, "We're the greatest in the land".

Medbh Peavoy, Eire

2) Why Leeds?

It's April 1970, I'm eight years old and living in Dublin. My father is interested in most sports and plays a lot of rugby union and cricket but football is not really his game. As such I don't have a family influence in either supporting a team or even watching football.

That is until the FA Cup Final and I sit down to watch it with my mother on our black and white television. My mum decides we will have a small bet on the outcome of the match so she says she will bet a shilling (5p) on Chelsea. Knowing little about football I reply that I will bet on the team in the dark shirts. She laughs and tells me that the team in the dark shirts is Chelsea so I will have to bet on the team in the white shirts...Leeds United.

Such is fate. Despite losing the bet I have been a devoted and passionate supporter for the thirty four years since. Looking back I'm just glad it didn't happen a year earlier or I could be supporting Leicester or Manchester City!

Neil Metchette, Eire

Hello from Brazil

Although I was born in Hull in 1961, I guess being a Leeds fan was in my blood and that was all there was to it. My first major disappointment as a Leeds fan came when Leeds lost to Chelsea in the 1970 FA Cup Final. I remember preparing to watch the game/s on tv and making myself some Leeds flags and banners out of paper to wave like the Leeds fans did at Wembley! I ended up in tears after the second replay and I remember some kids teasing me about it when I went to school carrying my shiny yellow Leeds bag.

I can honestly say that when Leeds did win the Cup against Arsenal in 1972 that it was one of the happiest days of my life. Even when I see the highlights of this game today and Leeds lifting the trophy it brings tears to my eyes.

The Cup Final that followed in '73 just stunned me as I'm sure it did every Leeds (and non Leeds) fan at the time. It was just so unbelievable that Leeds lost to such an (on paper) inferior team. It was so tragic. The memory of Montgomery's save of Peter Lorimer's 'unmissable' shot and Porterfield's goal are something that seem to haunt me like so many of Leeds 'almost, but not quite' moments in their history. Sunderland deserved it on the day though. Leeds United's league title in 1974 was another high point in my 'school life'. I remember asking my parents to buy me some Leeds sock tags, Number 1 as I was a goalkeeper. Whenever I played I wore them proudly. I also remember having football magazine pictures of the Leeds team and players all over my bedroom walls.

My whole world at that time was football and I really wanted to be a professional goalkeeper but it was not to be. Eventually, I got a teaching diploma and after taking a six-week holiday in Brazil I decided that I would like to go back and teach there. So I returned in 1986 to teach English to Brazilians.

Supporting Leeds at that time in Brazil was very difficult as there was no internet, so I could only find out what was going on by reading the local papers for the results. The only other way of finding out a bit more was by asking my mum to send me newspaper cuttings on the games, etc. So when Leeds were Division 1 Champions in 1992, I was probably the last Leeds fan on earth to find out we had won it. After all it takes on average one week to get a letter from England!

During the 18 years I've been in Brazil so far I've met very few English people here at all. The first one I remember meeting was in fact a Sunderland fan (who said the Devil doesn't exist?) who was working temporarily in a local factory and who would turn up at my house several times a week precisely at lunchtime!

When my daughter was born I had her christened with a LEEDS badge in her white dress pocket, whilst I wore my Leeds shirt at the ceremony. Soon after, when Leeds beat Lazio in the Champion's

FANTHOLOGY

League one-nil with a wonderful Smith goal such was my delight that I jumped up off the bed to shout 'Goal!' but had forgotten in all the excitement that I was holding my sleeping, week-old daughter. She rolled across the bed like the ball rolled along the grass into the back of Lazio's net! My daughter wouldn't stop screaming for hours and my wife didn't stop screaming at me for days.

On the day Leeds played Galatasaray in the second leg of the UEFA Cup I couldn't concentrate on anything all day long except for the big game. When I went out in the car before it to pick the wife up I found I couldn't park my Ford Fiesta even in a space large enough to park a bus, I was just too anxious about the match. Finally, I found a parking space big enough in the city centre to park two buses but, as I reversed, I scraped down the side of a car scratching it all...then seeing there wasn't much time left before kick off, I did the only decent thing I could think of...I drove off!

Over the years I've bought lots of Leeds souvenirs. I have three photos of Elland Road on the wall of the room at home which I use for teaching. There's also a framed certificate of Leeds shares I bought years ago. I use English teaching books which mention the city of Leeds in them and waste no time at all to explain to my students everything they want, and don't want, to know about Leeds, the city and the team.

There are three pubs in São Paulo, 40 miles from where I live and when I go in them I always wear a Leeds shirt. Once I dragged the wife out of bed early one Sunday morning to drive her to one of these pubs because the Leeds game would be shown live on tv at 8 o'clock in the morning. In the pub I was lucky enough to meet another Leeds fan called Charles who had recently arrived in Brazil. We all watched the game, had an 'English breakfast' and drank Guinness.

Nowadays, I always listen to the Leeds games on Radio Aire on the internet and I email them several times during every game. They always read my name out during the broadcast and must be sick of hearing from me! I'm a member of the official Leeds site and often post messages on it. I'm also a member of two other fan clubs called waccoe and motforum which I regularly post to as well. One of my friends from the motforum, called Graham, but who is known as California White because he lives in the USA, came to visit us last year. He supped a fair amount of Skol and sang all the Leeds songs he knew at the top of his voice in a pizza restaurant. No need to say a good time was had by all.

I'm not ashamed to admit that I broke out in tears while listening to the Bolton-Leeds match which got them relegated. Some might say it's only a game, but Leeds United are part of me, like family, and it hurts deep inside when we lose and much more so to be relegated. What do people here think of my Leeds fanaticism? Well, if it's anything to go by, my wife thinks I'm nuts. I think the other people are just too polite to say so.

Ian Bloom, Brazil

My life since Leeds United

Why Leeds? I'm always asked the same question...It was like falling in love...There's no real reason for it, apart from Leeds United being the best team in the world ever. On television I saw them play 1860 Munich in the Champions' League qualifier some years ago and when I saw Leeds play Chelsea, again on telly, I lost my heart to them. I admired their style. And that was indeed the beginning of a great football love. To be honest, I hadn't really been interested in that round-ball game before!

FANTHOLOGY

I followed the games via television firstly, up to the UEFA Cup match versus PSV Eindhoven. My mate and I then decided to travel to Leeds for the first time to watch the next round of the UEFA Cup, the quarter final! We organised a flight to Leeds/Bradford Airport, booked hotel rooms for a few days, took some days off work and had the Leeds ticket office's guarantee to have match tickets reserved. Unfortunately the team didn't reach the quarter finals but having booked and paid in advance we went for the famous, so-called 'empty-stadium-tour'!

In Leeds for the first time, I was really impressed with what a nice town it was and how friendly the people were. Admittedly I have to confess that I didn't understand a word they were saying. Initially, I had to get used to the accent. On my first time in the North the best conversation I had was with two deaf guys in 'The Three Legs' whilst watching United on telly. Leeds had a Premier League match on that Sunday afternoon, the day we had to fly back to Munich, so we couldn't get to that game either.

Because I was so eager to see our boys, we travelled to Thorp Arch, which really was not easy to find! But after a little odyssey we arrived at the training ground. I guess we were lucky that we hadn't been arrested, because we passed a prison opposite a few times which could have left a strange/wrong impression until we finally found it. But it was too late by then. I could see some big cars with dark panes coming by and passing us, inside one of them was Mark Viduka. Training was definitely finished for the day. As a construction worker told us later, they only train in the morning... Bad luck again, but at least I could take some pictures of Elland Road. Inside the ground as well. I am slim enough to squeeze through the stadium barriers. Sadly my friend Ingo had to stay out rather than get stuck between the doors.

124

A TOUR OF THE WORLDWIDE WHITES

We were more lucky the following season. As we had to play Hapoel Tel Aviv in the UEFA Cup it was a good occasion to attend the match live because it took place in Florence and I love Italy anyway. My first international away game! Great! I loved it. And what a fantastic result: four Alan Smith goals after we had allowed an early one against us.

I didn't know any Leeds fans up until then but met some guys in an Italian bar after the match, especially one who had lost his mates (Gary). After a few beers, my pal and I brought him back to Florence's city centre. Near our hotel was an Irish pub. We were about a hundred metres away from it when Gary cried out, 'Ooh, I can hear the boys!' And indeed the place was packed with Leeds fans singing football chants. I absolutely loved the hilarious atmosphere, the more so as I'm a child of happiness myself. It seemed to be one big family. I got to know Leeds-mad people from England, Norway and Belgium. Some of them are still friends of mine, especially the two Belgium lads, Kris and Ziggi. We met again for the next round of the UEFA Cup in Málaga, went to several Leeds games in England and they also visited me for ground hopping in Munich; Olympia Stadium, Gruenwalder Stadium (the former and recent 1860's ground), Sportpark Unterhaching. Ziggi and Kris joined the Kippax Leeds fans and after that night in Italy it didn't take long for my mate Ingo and I to become members of them, too.

The Leeds United Supporters' Club Munich was founded on the 1st of June 2002 in Rome. That's when I started to run my Leeds website. We are just some friends that meet up to watch Leeds United games on tv or travel to matches or just have a pint and a laugh. We are all Germans except for a couple of English Leeds supporters who live in Munich.

FANTHOLOGY

My first home match was against Man U when we won 1-0 by a famous Harry Kewell goal. I'd never been to an English football ground before that match and I had a seat in the second row! How near to the pitch that was! Unimaginable in German stadiums. No barriers or fences between you and the players. Lucas Radebe was smiling at me as I took his picture! And I got goose pimples the whole match long... Now I feel at home at Elland Road, always meet some friends there and have my regular Guinness with Coller in the Supporters' Club, but it's always very special for me to be there!

I watch Leeds United matches as often as possible. That means I travel to England a few times a year. Unfortunately the flight to Leeds/Bradford Airport is very expensive from Munich, so at times I take my chance to get a rather cheap connection to London to watch our boys play. I missed one game that was shown on tv because I was skiing in Austria that weekend and there was no pub with Sky Sports on in the whole area. It was a terrible defeat so I hadn't to suffer that much as I always suffer when we lose a game.

I nearly missed Fulham at home when I drove back from a trip to Vienna and my car broke down. I didn't give a damn about my car, but was absolutely annoyed that I mightn't be able to watch my team. I got home to Munich by train and finally arrived at 'The Outland', an Australian bar - but the landlord is from Wolverhampton, where my mates had been waiting for me and texting me about what was happening on the pitch, the goals, yellow cards and so on. I was just in time for Fulham's equaliser and then the vital Matteo goal. We had a half-night celebration afterwards and the inevitable hangover the next day.

I'm fortunate to have nice colleagues at work who know about my addiction to the club. My office has Leeds posters and pictures everywhere and every now and then you can hear 'Marching on

Together' sounding across the hall and they are very understanding. First question each Monday is, 'How did Leeds play this weekend?' But I also had to suffer loads of schadenfreude from them when Leeds went down and my second team, 1860 Munich, too and even the football club from my native town who were relegated to the third Bundesliga. Sharp tongues claim that I should become a Bayern Munich supporter to get them relegated eventually!

In Munich it's unusual not to follow 1860 or FC Bayern and it's even more unusual to support an English team and it's most unusual when it's Leeds United as there's a majority of Man U fans! So in most of Munich's bars I'm known as a massive Leeds fan by the staff and the guests, especially by the British ones. A barkeeper in an Irish pub once told me I was the greatest Leeds supporter he'd ever seen in Munich. That was a huge compliment for me since that pub is mostly frequented by Brits, with Leeds fans amongst them!

Since I've known that Nicky Byrne played for Leeds as a goalkeeper one of my favourite bands is now Westlife. Embarrassing I know, but they have really got a few good songs. I listen to Radio Aire whenever I get my notebook connected to the net. I deeply enjoy it - even if it hurts a bit to be so far away from Leeds.

A few weeks ago I was talking to a young guy from the south of England, who had problems with my strong Leeds accent - what a compliment that was too!

MARCHING ON TOGETHER!

Ines Hoehbauer, Germany

FANTHOLOGY

Rock Fan

Scott from Gibraltar here. I'm seventeen and I've supported the Mighty Whites for around twelve years. I began supporting them when I saw them on telly as my dad was watching. Since then I've been collecting shirts, programmes and autographs of players from the greatest club in the world.

I have a clear memory of watching the men in white in the Coca Cola Cup Final which we lost to Aston Villa but my personal highlight was watching Leeds v Pompey in the FA Cup 3rd Round at Fratton Park in '96 when we won 5-1.

Scott Pritchett, Gibraltar

USA! USA!

Mention football anywhere in the United States and more often than not you'll be drawn into a conversation about the relative merits of the prevent defense or the current wild card race. Of course, football in America means Gridiron - American Football, but in the Deep South it's even more complicated. Despite being the largest city in the South, the talk in the sports bars of Atlanta rarely revolves around the latest news of the Atlanta Falcons, or the incredibly successful baseball team, or the excitingly fresh-faced ice hockey team, and certainly not the woeful basketball team - it's college football. Fierce family fan rivalries are played out each year between September and January, when crowds in the region of 100,000 people turn up to watch a bunch of students play games. Their relative merits are debated ad-nausea. The only thing more popular, with the possible exception of firearms, is Church. Sound strange? Certainly, but that's what being a Leeds fan marooned in the Redneck Bible Belt and college football heartland is like - strange.

Atlanta describes itself as a world class city, but has virtually no history before 1850 and like most of America is superbly insular. To its credit it does boast four or five relatively authentic 'British' pubs, and it's to one of these oases that the ex-pats gravitate on match days. The pubs offer a respite from American sports. This week, the self-styled 'Worldwide leader in Sports' tv channel, ESPN, has delighted us with The National Spelling Bee competition, Putt-Putt, better known as Crazy Golf and the National Skipping Rope Finals, and for a few brief hours they replicate home for their patrons. Take last season's home game against Fulham, fairly typical of when we have the luxury of Leeds appearing live on American tv.

Having negotiated the dreadfully complicated tv listings, taken into account the time differences and made all the necessary telephone calls and emails, the 'Atlanta Whites' meet at Fado's Irish bar, the current favourite of Atlanta's British footy fans. The pub will generally attract around fifteen to twenty hardcore fans for every game, with more or less depending on the games being televised. For an important England game there might be a couple of hundred that come out of the woodwork, but for the most part it's a fairly select group. Leeds are well represented with seven regulars, the usual sprinkling of Arsenal, Man U, Chelsea, Liverpool, a few others such as Wolves, Everton and today, even a Fulham fan. Here's the next strange thing. Despite all the potential unpleasantness between this disparate group of rivals there is a begrudging comradeship that also exists. As much as it may be difficult to sit down next to a Manchester fan at the bar, with both of you wearing your colours and footy on the tv, there exists some weird kind of bond. You both yearn for home and understand each other's desire to be watching the game in your real local rather than this artificial haven.

So, at 11 am EST (Eastern Standard Time) the 'Atlanta Whites' are assembled at the bar staring at the screen showing a distinctly grey and chilly looking Elland Road on a winter's afternoon. Today we have a full house, with the only absentee, Carpet Entrepreneur, Charlie Armitage who is actually at the game! There's the Marshalls, Rob from Essex, Paul 'The Pope' McGowan, Gerry Gafford - the other American raised on a diet of late 60's and early 70's Leeds in Memphis and Mississippi, Nick, Mark Hutton, a Leeds native who's been working in the States for five years, and myself.

Local licensing laws prevent the sale of beer until 12.30 on a Sunday so the early consumption revolves around coffee rather than Harp, Guinness or Bass, but a few choose the traditional fry up that the pub offers too. As the game gets underway the crowd has swelled to a healthy twenty or so, but there is a distinctly sombre mood. The thought of Leeds at home to Fulham proves to be somewhat less than compelling for the neutrals and the Leeds contingent are reflecting on the prospect of a must-win game in mid-December against the backdrop of what appears to be a half empty Elland Road. As the game unfolds and Leeds take a 2-0 lead, talk turns to each other's progress in the Yahoo fantasy leagues, another staple of the 'soccer' starved ex-pat community. A brace from Saha brings mixed emotions in the bar, a yelp from the lone Fulham fan, groans of disbelief from the Atlanta Whites as talk turns to certain relegation, and amusement from the rest of the neutrals who are revelling in the plight of one of the most hated clubs around the world.

Of course, Dominic Matteo lifts the gloom, optimism is restored and all is well in Deep South once more. The bar starts serving beer and for a brief hour or so after the match you really could imagine that you are standing in the Adelphi or the Peacock. The final strange event comes to pass as the assembled throng disperses. Walking out of the relative authenticity of Fado's into bright Atlanta sunshine, 4,500 miles from home always causes a sudden jolt of weirdness to pass through the mind. Beeston it ain't. Another week must pass before most of us will be together again, this time for the Man City Monday night game. Of course, Monday night means Monday afternoon and a three o'clock kick off on the Eastern Seaboard. Fancy that, a three o'clock kick off, perhaps it'll feel more like home next time?

Adrian Dingle, USA

Lancaster, Pennsylvania

I've been asked the question 'Why Leeds?' so many times over the past decade they'll probably put it on my gravestone! Growing up in an American society which just assumes that 'soccer' is boring and its fans are mostly hooligans, I openly mocked the game for years, though like most of my friends I'd never really taken time to watch it. But I'd always had a passion for sports, and during six-month work stints in Derby and Oxford in 1991 and 1994/95, I decided I was missing a vital part of English culture by not at least going to a match.

I went to see Oxford v York in January 1995, and to my surprise found that not only did I not feel in fear for my life, the experience was actually rather enjoyable. I soon started going to other matches: at Oxford, Nottingham Forest, Spurs, and so on, but although I was becoming a convert to the sport, nowhere seemed like 'home' to me.

Then in March of 1995, I went to Elland Road for the first time, to see Leeds United play Sheffield Wednesday. Leeds were dreadful, losing a dour 1-0 match on a Chris Waddle goal and squandering something like 18 corners, but I suspected I would be back. The stadium, the support, the city, the northern 'grit'... everything just 'felt' like home to me. Two weeks later, I went to see Leeds play away to Forest...a comprehensive 3-0 defeat in which Leeds were repeatedly victimized by Forest counter-attacks. But with this I was definitely hooked! This was 'my' team, and I was back to Elland Road again just three weeks later, though it would be a while before I'd see us win for the first time.

The passion only grew once I returned to the States, and soon I started planning annual UK holidays around the fixture list. Ten seasons later, I've now been back to another twenty or so of our matches, witnessing everything from Yeboah wonder goals to relegation and I have seen us on tv or heard us on radio countless times. I keep abreast of the club news on a daily basis, have enough club paraphernalia to fill a room and have adopted the city like it's my own, even giving tours to a few of my skeptical British friends!

Win or lose, I'm Leeds -and proud of it - for life.

Matthew Tharp, USA

Norwegian Would

I guess I'm Leeds partly because of my dad and because of Tony Yeboah. My dad is a Leeds fan, and I grew up in a small place in the north of Norway, so my dad had all the influence on me when it came to football. It was back in the days when you could watch English top football on the Norwegian channel named NRK, which everyone had, and my dad was watching Leeds v

Wimbledon. I sat down to watch and after a while Tony Yeboah comes from nowhere and scores this magnificent goal. He took the ball down on his chest, then his thigh, and volleyed it, hitting the bar, bouncing down on the ground and up in the goal. After that I loved Yeboah, and since he played for Leeds, I loved Leeds...and I still do, and I always will.

Even though I live in Norway and have never been to Leeds, I love Leeds more than any team here in Norway, all because of one goal when I was young.

Andreas Svenby, Norway

Oystein

For many older Leeds United supporters in Norway, it all began in 1965, when Leeds lost to Liverpool in the Cup Final. The underdogs, the beaten team, became their favourites. I was born the following year, 1966, and grew up in the small city of Haugesund on the west coast of Norway. My family didn't have a tv set at home until the mid seventies so I did not grow up watching the top English teams like we can do now. I have no older brothers - or sisters. I mention this because a lot of my mates inherited their favourite team from an older brother. My father took me to local footy, at the time Vard Haugesund were really big in Norway. They reached the Norwegian Cup Final in 1975. He supported Man U but never, fortunately, tried to convince me about that team.

My support for Leeds started in 1974 when I was eight. My mate Olav didn't do like 'everybody' else did and select the older brother's favourite side, he selected Leeds United. So did my nine-year-old cousin, Jostein and I was very much influenced by him at the time. After that there was never any doubt. There was never any other team.

Just a couple of years back, my mother found a 'weapon-shield' that I had drawn as a child. I had forgotten all about it, of course. It had a lot of crests on it, and the words 'LEEDS ØYSTEIN LEEDS' on the top and 'Billy Bremner' at the bottom. As far as I could remember, Peter Lorimer was my favourite from my first years with Leeds, but this drawing documented that I couldn't remember the very start of following Leeds or exactly when it began. Thanks mum!

I was a proud collector of the Shoot magazines, and some Norwegian football magazines, and the Leeds United pictures were all over the walls in my bedroom. I can't mention the names of the players, because it's not possible without tears coming...a wonderful time it was, back then.

My first Leeds United souvenir was a gym bag, the Eiffel Tower was on it, and the result of THAT match in '75. But it was a Leeds bag and I proudly used it as much as I could. My first Leeds strip was the Admiral yellow away strip from 76/77, with white and blue on the arms. I was ten by then, and I still have it, of course. My father visited England in the autumn 1977, and brought home to me a Leeds United silk scarf, a couple of crests, a Leeds medallion and more. At this time, I had also started to learn English, and it was easier to follow Leeds knowing the language. I was able to read about them in English magazines and papers, not just browsing the pictures. We also collected those cards from chewing gum packets. I switched cards with friends when I had two of the same. Finally I had some hundred cards, including all the Leeds players. One day I sold all my collection to a mate; I'm still angry with myself that I didn't save the LUFC cards.

A TOUR OF THE WORLDWIDE WHITES

Being older, other interests took my time, playing the game myself, playing guitar, education, computers, marriage, car and house. But Leeds was always there in my heart.

Before the time of satellite tv, I used to listen to BBC Radio 5 every Saturday. The signals were poor and noisy, but I was able to follow the games live. I also joined the supporters club, Leeds United Supporters Club of Scandinavia, LUSCOS. For almost ten years now I have contributed to the LUSCOS magazine, The Peacock News, a magazine sent to more than **3,000** members seven times a year.

I finally gave economic priority to my first visit to Leeds in August 1995, at the age of 29. It was enormous just to visit Elland Road! I cried when I caught my first glimpse of the stadium, at lunchtime ahead of the Liverpool game. And visiting the stadium, seeing the pictures, cups, I just can't describe it. Naturally, I went wild in the Leeds Collection - the name of the supporters' shop at the time!

Since the first trip, I have been able to see about twenty Leeds United games live, both home and away. I have had a Strikers' card every season from 1996, to be able to get tickets in the away end for the odd game, with all the Leeds fans. A typical trip for me went as follows:

From my diary - August 1997:
Sheffield Wednesday, away - having arrived in England, I was on my way to St. Pancras Station ticket office fully kitted out. I had agreed to meet Rob there but I'd never met him before other than via internet. I was waiting for the green light to cross the street, when I noticed a person looking at me from the other side of the road. Later Rob said, 'You looked so lost, it had to be you...'

FANTHOLOGY

Highlight - just to sit in the Leeds crowd at an away game for the very first time. I was in a fit of Norwegian-White ecstasy, saying, 'Oh, this is great!' about every five seconds! I of course tried to sing along, take part in chants etc., too!

Crystal Palace: Met a lot of Leeds fans in the Adelphi pub in Leeds, had 'Lucky Lasagne' - never to be repeated - not because of the quality of food, but the 'luck' which followed it. Was seated in the Family Stand at Elland Road, together with my former wife, my son Torleif, and a Norwegian couple - friends of ours.

Highlight - you could almost touch the grass from the Family Stand, great view.

Lowlight - After seeing Norwegian Gunnar Halle struggling for 30 minutes, having to say to a person behind me, and I honestly meant it, 'Norwegians should be in the crowd, not on the pitch!' But most of all, not being able to celebrate a goal with Torleif. That was disappointing, it was!

***

Liverpool, home:
Highlight - Seated in the Kop, for the very first time.
I left UK somewhat disappointed, yes. 3 of 9 points, I had hoped for 7! I can't say I'm too angry, because there is more to my relationship with LU than just wanting to watch good footy and celebrate glory days. Nevertheless seeing them playing well would be very much appreciated...

Mette and I married on August 4th 2001. She is a beautiful woman and we have a lot in common including a passion for football. She is a Leeds supporter as much as anyone else, and told me she would love to travel to see them play. I planned to propose to her at Elland Road, but she beat me to that. I changed my plans, and in my wedding speech to her I told her about the plans for our honeymoon, and gave her a Striker's card with her name on it.

Once we were in Leeds we did the stadium tour, paid for as a wedding present from the club! I think the most interesting thing for Mette was the dressing rooms, then walking out through the tunnel. The icing on the cake for this special day was the three course lunch. We got Nike's executive box on the top of East Stand. It was fabulous! A wonderful table for two was prepared, flowers on the table, menu cards printed for just the two of us and napkins formed as home shirts. And the most lovely restaurant view you can imagine - the Elland Road ground getting prepared for the league opening against Southampton (cutting the grass, marking the lines, etc. - a lot of busy people out there).

I picked some local food; i.e. Starter: Whitby crab and prawn salad, roast sirloin of beef with Yorkshire pudding and vegetables, and for dessert; apple pie and Wensleydale cheese. Finally we had tea and coffee with mints (the chocolate was wrapped in blue paper with LU logo). A lovely meal in lovely surroundings - and the greatest hospitality I have experienced. Even Heather, who I had booked with, came by to say hello and see if everything was okay! After the meal we spent a fortune in the Leeds United Collection, had a pint at the Old Peacock, and took the bus back to town.

I feared a 0-0 draw, and was relieved and delighted when the first goal came. Mette could celebrate another Leeds win, and keep her 100%, 2-0 win record (okay, only her second game, but nevertheless....) In the match day programme she could read: 'Dear Mette, this spot was intended for my proposal, but you beat me to that. Anyway, I just want to say I love you and that I am delighted to take you to Leeds and Elland Road for our honeymoon. Enjoy the game, sweetheart. Marching on together, yours 4ever. Øystein.'

Back in London, Arsenal was Mette's first away game, and my second. We finished with only 9 men. What an atmosphere it is at away games! We only used our seat for a couple of minutes in the break. It was more than electric when we scored, and the best chants of the day were 'Same old Arsenal, always cheating' and 'Let's go effing mental!'

When back in Norway, I see live games on telly as much as possible. The past few years, some supporters in Haugesund have met in a local pub to see the games. We have our names and our own signs on the seats like 'Leeds United supporter no.1' etc. For games not selected by Sky Sports, I listen to Radio Aire via internet. The internet really is a good way to follow your team from overseas, both in terms of official news and meeting other supporters. I have been a member of the Leeds United email list for many years, and met a lot of great people, both on the net and in real life. There is no doubt that internet and the mailing list has brought me a lot closer to Leeds and made it possible to increase my knowledge and follow the team better than before.

These days, with satellite tv, Norwegian pubs show games from Sky Sports and others. There are even pubs labelling themselves as sports pubs or football pubs, where shirts and scarves decorate the walls and ceiling, and with both big screens and a lot of tv sets in every direction. The only thing they don't have is the real ale - a pint of bitter isn't achievable in Norway, unfortunately!

A TOUR OF THE WORLDWIDE WHITES

My two sons have heard a slow version of "Marching on Together", both verses and chorus, as part of their lullaby since they were born and I collect lyrics to the Leeds United songs; both recorded music and chants from the terraces. I even have a website just for that. Says my friend John Boocock about the Leeds United songbook on the web, 'You're on the bus to Elland Road, you're up the back of the Kop, you're in the away end at Highbury, you're on top of Pen-Y-Ghent or you're sat half cut in the armchair with the telly flickering. You want to sing, you want to sing a song that you love, a song of high endeavour. Blast! You don't know all the words.' This site will attempt to fulfil the needs of all the Leeds fans who have been condemned to mumbling after the first verse/chorus of a great big-throated roar from the Pride of Yorkshire.

In the summer of 2004, Leeds supporters all over the world were waiting for a new season to start. This time, a season in the second division, for the first time in 14 years. Were we influenced by that fact? The answer is NO! Deep inside ourselves remains the true love for Leeds United. It's still worth it to spend the equivalent of a season ticket to travel over from Norway for the odd game. We will continue to go to the pub to see Leeds live on Sky, and write columns for the Peacock News. We will still buy new shirts. We are still Leeds!

Mette, Torleif (8), Joakim (5) and myself set off on our very first pre-season tour July 11th, Sunday, early in the morning. We left Haugesund, Norway in our VW Golf with Leeds roses in the back window with our nose pointed at Boden, Sweden. The kids were brilliant in the back-seat and we actually reached Sweden on the first day of driving. Found a hotel in Torsby, just across the border. On Monday we drove to Umeå, another 8.5 hours in the car, and the final stage to Boden on Tuesday was a short one, completing the 20.5 hours of driving, 1650 kilometres from home.

We stayed at the Bodensia Inn, where also the players stayed. It actually didn't take long before spotting the first Leeds United players. Fortunately they wore team colours, because all faces but three were brand new! It really did take some time to recognize the lads - who was who?! Anyway; Torleif and Joakim collected autographs big time, and on-trial player Hignett and brand new skipper Butler were in the book after a few minutes in Boden, to be followed by another 10-11 names during the stay. It was hard to get the book complete because, with two kids on holiday, we just couldn't go to every training session.

We had a wonderful time in Sweden, not only because of the place but because all of us really enjoyed watching the lads of Leeds; talking to them, taking pictures, watching them at the training field, and of course during those two games. Torleif was quite good at asking, 'Autograph please' in English, and also remembering a lot of names/faces; and Joakim always remembered to say, 'Thank you,' after each signature in his book. Joakim meeting Joachim was of course another highlight!

Of all players and staff we talked to, I was impressed with how positive they were to us. They took their time for autographs, pictures and a chat, and were also really nice with both kids and adults.

After the game in Piteå ended on Saturday July 17th at 6.05-ish pm, we decided to drive to Haugesund to watch our local team, Vard Haugesund, Norwegian Division One, the next day. We had less than twenty-four hours to kick off, and 1600 kilometres to drive. Eighteen hours in the car, with a couple of breaks on the way and even time for a shower at home and going to the pub, then to watch Vard win 4-3 against Raufoss in a thriller of a game. Don't you dare say we're part-timers!

The next trip to Elland Road is already booked, as is membership in Forever Leeds for all the family. It would take more than financial problems, bad board decisions, change of managers or relegation to break our relation to Leeds United. Actually, I believe we will be marching on together, at least until the world stops going 'round'

Øystein Bjøndal Lund, Norway

And finally, an antipodean email to Relish Books.

>Well, when I read you wanted an anthology BY Leeds fans I thought, 'Who amongst us is capable of stringing four lines together and getting the last one to rhyme?' then thought, 'Naaaaaa!'

>You see we ain't poetic. Never have been, never will be. If someone hadn't thought up MOT, we'd still be sat in front o' telly saying, 'He's trash, blimey! I could do better than that.'

>But if you want some stories then go to our web site and see if any of these will do.

>Cheers, Adelaide Whites (Swags)

Eh? Our Aussie mates might want to check the meaning of 'anthology' next time, bless 'em!

My Top 10 Places In and Around Elland Road

The Kop in the 80's when it was terraced - I watched my first game at Elland Road from there.

FANTHOLOGY

Wesley Street - first sight of the ground after a 3hr+ drive from London each fortnight.

Lowfields Road Terraces (the pens in the late 80's/ early 90's) - liveliest part of the ground for many seasons.

Front Row of the Kop - cracking close up view and deafening noise when a Leeds goal goes in.

South Stand Upper in the 80's - what a noise we used to make, the best acoustics in the ground.

For sentimental reasons, the old Club Shop on Elland Road by the training pitches - the old hut is still there after all these years.

The Billy Bremner Statue - a reminder of the Glory years. Can't pass it by without feeling some sadness.

West Stand Paddock by the tunnel and dugouts - great watching the managers and coaches barking out instructions from the touchline.

The Peacock - great sing songs, especially prior to Man U Matches.

Lowfields Stand in the 80's - a great old stand which is in so many old clips of the great Leeds games of the 70's.

MW

Chapter 5

Memorable occasions, crucial games

Not all matches burn themselves in the memory - some are instantly forgettable but when they are memorable, the details are as fresh today as the day they happened.

In autumn 1968 Leeds opened the new Spion Kop to replace the old, uncovered one. Many league grounds had spion kops, the name deriving from a sloping hill in South Africa, scene of a battle where the red-coated British unsuccessfully attempted to remove the Boers, whose homeland it was.

We will fight, fight, fight for U-ni-i-ted

A full 90 minutes before kick off, the entire terrace was a seething mass of bodies. Manchester United fans were trying to take our Kop.

We had known something extra-special was happening before we rushed up the stairs to take our places. There had been an electric tension in the air as my mate and I hurried down Lowfields Road along with the gathering fans. Excitement and the nervous chatter churned my stomach whilst our fast walk kept threatening to break into a run. The mighty new stand beckoned. It was our new fortress, barely a year old. Home fans had said goodbye to the cramped Scratching Shed on Elland Road. Away fans were welcome to it now.

143

FANTHOLOGY

The mood had grown more intense as we joined huge, snaking queues with the vast array of Leeds scarves, white with those distinctive blue and gold bands, proudly displaying allegiance. Deep in the midst, over two hours before the start, we pressed forward, eager, anxious to get in, afraid the gates would lock us out, forcing us to miss the unmissable. Huge shouts from within made us even more desperate to be inside. Queuing, we were driven to the edge of panic as rumours spread that Man United fans were there, on the Kop. Some said they had taken it, like Everton fans had once taken the Stretford End itself. Anger and frustration swept the tide forward, making the turnstile the magic gateway. Six-deep narrowed to four, to two and then we were in.

However great the tension was outside, it became almost overwhelming once through those turnstiles. Though a few lingered around the entrances, we were bursting to get up the steps and on to the terraces and play our part in the struggle, shouting and singing Leeds on to victory. The enemy were at hand and we were needed.

Normally, that early before kick off, there was still plenty of room. Not today. As we turned the corner to make our way up the terrace, we were stunned to find it already full to bursting. Looking up I could see a vast bank completely split into two sections: one wearing white, yellow and blue, the other wearing the loathsome red and white. A double line of police was all that separated us from the Man U. fans who had had the daring, the nerve, the cheek to invade our territory. Talk was that tons of them had run across the pitch from the Scratching Shed to join up with the Manchester fans already here. Someone said they'd trashed The Peacock pub causing it to be shut down. We could see loads of them being chucked out of the ground, a lot of them wearing crash helmets. We burrowed in to the crowd trying to move at least a little way up our side of the Kop as lighters, coins, cans, anything that might hurt whizzed through the air, aimed at the opposition. The nearer the back of the stand it came from, the faster and more dangerous it was.

Sweltering heat, the conflict and aggression, and being in the heart of a surging, swaying throng gave me a real tinge of fear but, much more than that, it was incredibly exciting.

Chants fired up towards the roof and away, proclaiming who we loved, strengthening our resolve whilst trying to intimidate them. 'United' they'd proclaim. 'Leeds' we'd explode back, skilfully timing it so we reclaimed our full title of Leeds United, denying their 'there's only one United' boasts. 'Part time supporters', intended to mock our failure to show up in force at Old Trafford, was met with 'Back to school on Monday'. We have jobs, our retort was saying. That's why we can't travel away. But sung most often and with most vitriol was either 'We-hate-**Man**/ches/ter', or 'We will **fight, fight, fight** for U-ni-i-ted, till we win the Football League. To hell with Man U-ni-i-ted… ' and we sang that with real pride because it was already true, we had just won it for the very first time. We were the League Champions..

Though we had managed to squeeze a little way up the Kop, we were still too low for any protection from missiles. You had to keep your hands tensed all the time, pointing upwards like buffers towards the shoulders of the person in front. That was the only way to cope with the constant pushing and shoving. Worst was when I was looking over towards the Man U. fans and saw a dark brown, quart bottle hurtling through the air, heading straight for me. As well as 'Bulmers', I thought it had my name on it. Being sardine-packed in the crowd, it was too late to raise my hands. Self-protection was impossible. Cringing, I braced myself for impact but a split-second before it hit, some poor beggar at my right shoulder thought it was the perfect moment to begin a chant for Leeds. He leaned forward and found, instead, it was only the perfect moment to collect a gashed head.

The bottle shattered against his temple, showering all around. He crumpled, or tried to crumple, but the surrounding supporters kept him upright. He had copped it full on the side of his head and blood was flowing freely through the fingers he clasped to the wound. The completely packed, sorry-can't-make-room-for-anybody crowd parted like the Red Sea when they saw a bloodstained man about to gush all over them. He was helped to the front and carted off by the St John's Ambulance squad, finally rewarded with work after years of inactivity. Instantly, the sea closed up again.

Conversation between my mate and I was minimal. On a day of such action, it was meaningless and we were absorbed into something much bigger. During a brief lull, I noticed the whole stadium was almost full to the brim and it was still forty minutes before the start. The only space I saw was around the Directors' Box where drinks would still be being swilled down on such a hot day. Crummy pop music, supposedly our pre-match entertainment, blasted from tannoys, failing entirely to pick up the warlike mood on the terraces. Everyone's attention was fixed on our battle of the Spion Kop.

I wasn't just a spectator but, like thousands more, a participant. We couldn't see why we had to stand in fear at our own ground. The Manchester fans weren't going to throw their weight around any more. We'd all had enough, didn't like being bullied. 'No one takes the Gelderd End,' we sang repeatedly and we meant it. To back this up, every few minutes there was a sudden increase in volume, the thunder of feet, gasps of excitement and shock as the Leeds fans nearest the enemy mounted a charge. Six times they charged, six times they were repulsed by a combination of Stretford Enders and the West Riding Constabulary. As kick off approached, the Man United fans, though there in large numbers and defiant, had been hemmed in.

Aching calf and thigh muscles, sore throats and thunderous applause greeted the two teams' arrival less than ten minutes before kick off. The game itself was only the second half of the whole contest. The Leeds players learned that when they found a third of the Kop booing them as they warmed up in front of it. The intensity of feeling had not changed but had found a new outlet. For now, the centre of the action moved to the pitch, with both teams being shouted on from under one roof.

Leeds led at the official 'half·time' thanks to an own goal by Sadler. No chance of a trip to the bog. Getting out would be difficult, getting back impossible. Just time to read in the programme: 'These are days of change for Manchester United, our very welcome visitors today.' Right about the change, WRONG about the welcome.

For the only time ever against Leeds, George Best did something, scoring twice in the second half. We were Champions, playing at home and far higher in the league than them. How mortifying to have thousands of their supporters entrenched on our Kop and how painful to find ourselves 2-1 down to an inferior team, for all its Best, Charlton and Kidd. Desperation fuelled our chants as the second half wore on. Playing towards us, Leeds mounted attack after attack, themselves desperate for an equaliser, as time ebbed away. Finally, it did arrive, scored with an outrageous overhead kick by who else but Billy Bremner. He neither could nor would ever let us down. The team's fantastic spirit was epitomised by his incredible effort. That spirit was being matched by us on the Kop. Euphoria, delirium led into repeated choruses of 'We shall not be moved' and then it happened. The Man United fans' nerve broke.

Realising that though the game was only drawn, the day was lost, they set about making a strategic retreat. We saw them start to push forward en masse heading for the bottom of the Kop and towards the pitch, a red and white lava flow, forcing fans to slide around them and fill the void left behind. We immediately spread across to our right, re-occupying the space vacated. Added to our happiness at the brilliant equaliser was now a joyous feeling of victory. The biggest insult you can throw at a team's fans had been rebuffed. We had reclaimed our territory, never to be seriously challenged again. Now we watched their retreat.

A pitch invasion seemed the likely intention as they spilled over the retaining fence but that did not happen. A twenty-yard space behind the goal had been left by setting the new stand back for further ground development. They filled that space and then turned round to taunt us, singing, 'We'll see you all outside...' before herding through a gateway at the corner. We mockingly waved them off then watched as a Lorimer thunderbolt was hit with such power that though Stepney saved it, it forced **him** into the net. Behind the Kop, skirmishes broke out after the game until the Man United supporters were driven off for good, leaving a trail of destruction on their way back to the station. The Evening Post was to hail United's 'fighting spirit' for that day, September 6th, 1969, the day we claimed the right to our own home.

Graeme Garvey

TOP 10 TROPHIES - WON

1   First Division Championship 1973/74
2   FA Cup 1972
3   First Division Championship 1968/69
4   First Division Championship 1991/92
5   Inter-Cities Fairs' Cup 1970/71
6   Inter-Cities Fairs' Cup 1967/68
7   League Cup 1968
8   Second Division Championship 1989/90
9   FA Charity Shield 1992
10   FA Youth Cup 1996/97

TOP 10 TROPHIES - MISSED

1   European Cup Final 1975
2   First Division Runners-Up 1971/72
3   FA Cup Final 1970
4   Cup-Winners' Cup 1973
5   First Division Runners-Up 1969/70
6   First Division Runners-Up 1970/71
7   FA Cup Final 1973
8   Coca-Cola Cup Final 1996
9   First Division Runners-Up 1965/66
10   First Division Runners-Up 1964/65

MW

FANTHOLOGY

Time for a confession...

LUFC Tales

1) Most people agree that Leeds' best badge was the 70's smiley design. Unfortunately, I have to admit my part in the change of that design. Look at any Elland Rd footage from the late 70's and you'll notice the corner flags with that smiley design.

I used to go down and watch training in the school holidays and one day managed to sneak into the ground. There, in the groundsman's room under the DJ box, were the four corner flags. How could an 11 year old resist claiming a unique piece of LUFC memorabilia? I nicked one, and the rest is history. The following season they changed the badge and our decline towards the Second Division began. I'm sure it was the fact that they only had three matching corner flags that prompted the change. I still have it today and reckon it must be worth something - watch out for it on Ebay!

More tales later, meanwhile, for fans, it is entirely possible that what happens on the way to or from a match eclipses the game itself. Travelling to a hostile Northern town or city, it is more than likely.

The Penguin Vultures

It was in the mid 80's and my mate Martin (the now 'Doctor') Whitehead, was a student at Durham University. Eccentric Frankie and me had this great idea to go spend the night in Durham with Dr Whitehead after taking in the away match at Newcastle. For me it was my first away game so I was a bit apprehensive and didn't say owt to me parents as Mum, especially, was the worrying type.

150

MEMORABLE OCCASIONS, CRUCIAL GAMES

We headed up Saturday morning on the National Express coach from Leeds and met Martin at the Gallowgate Bus Station close to the ground. We had no colours on but Martin was wearing a black donkey jacket and in his pocket was a Leeds scarf. You couldn't see it unless you stood at the side of him.

We made straight for the café in the station and it would be about 10.30am at this point. Some Geordie fans were in the café having some snap. Our Yorkshire accents were a dead giveaway but there was no hassle and all seemed well with the world. After breakfast down into the centre of town for a meander into the bookies for a bet and then we headed back up towards the ground.

Strange the things you remember. David Harvey was making his comeback game in goals for Leeds having had a spell at Vancouver Whitecaps and that was the name that stood out as we sat on a wall near the ground reading the match programme. Suddenly you felt a presence around you, the sort I experienced some years later on 42nd street in New York before Times Square was cleaned up. Eyes watching you, sussing you out like a leopard about to pounce on its dinner!

There were about eight Geordies gathered round us and the first one spoke, 'Where're you lads from, like?'

Martin in his best attempted Geordie accent uttered the fatal word 'Newcastle' but it came out sounding like 'Newt Hattle'. He then went on to explain that he was a student at Durham and that we were his mates who had come up for the weekend, the only problem being that the attempted Geordie accent was lost as he relayed the tale.

FANTHOLOGY

'What's that in yer pocket then?'

A difficult one for Martin to answer without giving the game away, so he proudly removed his Leeds scarf from the pocket. The Geordies took it and then proceeded to ask me to open my bomber jacket which I did but sadly for them they found no scarf or colours to nick. It's a shame they have to resort to this tactic I thought just because black and white are naff colours compared to the mighty Blue, White and Yellow but then so is their team. What we were all thinking in reality was that we were gonna get turned over big style. As it was they took the scarf and advised us to watch ourselves. They would let us off this time.

Nerves were now getting the better of us, adrenalin kicking in. Other groups had obviously seen this incident and we thought we better head away from the ground for our own safety. We walked off towards the town centre once more and soon we were on a street the equivalent of Briggate just after midday Saturday afternoon. Walking along three in a row we noticed some geezers following us, tattooed blokes, with fags and combat army trousers.

'Av any you lads got a light?' No response from Martin.

'Av you got a light?' No response from Frankie.

'Av you got a light?' one said turning to me.

I replied, 'No, sorry.'

'Aye cos you're a Leeds b.....d aren't yer?' he said swinging his leg my way to try and kick me in the Orchestral Stalls!

MEMORABLE OCCASIONS, CRUCIAL GAMES

I am ashamed to say that we ran but for a moment we had lost Frankie who had dived into the road but somehow got to the other side. Me and Martin found a copper on the street corner and explained our predicament. We were still worried about Frankie when he turned up a few minutes later, safe. It's fair to say that Frankie is a more seasoned campaigner when it comes to away games and he was very much angling for us to leave the copper and make our own way to the ground. Me and Martin had other ideas, observing the penguin-like vultures, in their Newcastle shirts, waiting to pounce the very moment we walked away.

Me, 'We're from Leeds and we have had some bother from the locals can you help us?'

'Well lads what you need to do is walk down here and right at the end, then left and it will bring you out at the train station where you can meet your lot arriving with the special and then be escorted to the ground.'

Not exactly what we were hoping for…the Penguin Vultures were massing now and if we strayed from the copper that would be it. I think he could smell the fear and in the end offered to escort us to the station, much to our relief. At the station was a small pocket of Leeds fans who had also made their own way up to Newcastle. One group claimed that one of their lads had been stabbed in a pub in Darlington on the way up and he was now in hospital. How true this was we will probably never know but it wasn't stopping them going to the game.

We were waiting at the station, pondering, when two coppers approached to establish how many people were waiting. Next thing, nineteen of us were piled into the back of a Black Mariah and escorted through the masses of Penguin Vultures to the away

153

end. Police Taxis R Us! At this point we all started to feel much safer but what was most amusing at the time was the Leeds fans vehemently giving the two-fingered salute out of the window as we drove through the opposing fans. Straight into the ground, Leazes Terrace, no messing.

Now you would think it was a case of all is well with the world again, get your meat pie and relax…if only. At the back of my mind and all through the game I was thinking…win or lose how do we get out of here safe at the end? This wasn't helped by the site of a Mohican in the adjacent terrace wearing a kilt. He looked a right meathead and he did not seem very happy to see us.

Most Leeds fans didn't turn up until quite late but once those from the football special arrived all sorts of characters emerged. The first guy I remember was in his fifties, tailored but scruffy jacket and a black eye. The sort of eye that the dead guy had in Hitchcock's 'The Birds', black to the extent that it isn't almost there, an obvious war trophy. He climbs the stairs to the terrace entrance, takes one look at their Kop end, singing, and says, 'Look at that *effing* lot they think they're hard but they din't wreck Derby,' and walks off. Real class. We just stood there laughing but I was thinking I hope we don't turn out like that!

Next up was a guy called Bedford from our old school who spotted Martin. Martin asked him how he was doing and Bedford said, 'I don't associate myself with anyone who stayed on at school,' and walked off.

The game ended 2-1 in favour of Newcastle. Keegan and McDermott were playing and sure enough Keegan got the winner. Paul Hart had headed our equaliser but as ever we couldn't hold on. Martin's scarf was duly set on fire in their main end and all that was left was to contemplate getting back to Durham. Fortunately Frankie bumped into a couple of lads from the Three Horse Shoes, Headingley circuit who had driven up in their van. They gave us a lift back to Durham and we made the best of the rest of the weekend.

At one stage, though, back in Durham we were walking over a bridge when this lad passed us with a Newcastle scarf. We all looked at one another and were having the same thought of let's shove him over the wall and into the river. The fact that we didn't was down to not wearing a tailored jacket, having a black eye, being 50 or having wrecked Derby.

Fond memories now but it was a while before I went to another away game.

Dave Weathers

LUFC Tales continued

2) In the 80's it was imperative that you knew your bus timetables. Failure to do so earmarked you as an away fan. I remember, as a fifteen year old, us walking along Boar Lane in our Pringle sweaters and Fila trackie tops, debating whether KG, the bouncer at Jacomellis would let us in. We were playing Man City that day and a group of older lads mistakenly sussed us as young Mancs. The standard conversation followed - 'Where you from?' , 'Prove it - What bus do you get to town?' Luckily we were all fully paid up members of the Leeds Metro crew and were able to reel off an impressive timetable from all parts of Leeds. Woe betide any posh kids who were taken to town by car....

3) When we were fifteen we joined the Service Crew. Unfortunately, they didn't know that, so didn't tell us where the 'meet' was for the game at Bolton. Therefore, me, Jonny and Neil turned up in Bolton City Centre on our own, decked out in our new diamond Pringles and Filas. We walked out of the station into a war zone, with plenty of action between the two firms resembling a load of Jimmy Tarbucks scrapping with Bjorn Borgs.

We didn't know who was who and ducked into a shop selling organs and sheet music. Unfortunately, we'd been sussed and before long about twenty lads with bowlcuts had their noses pressed to the window with a few bold ones entering the shop and giving us a sly dig. Our predicament was noticed by the manager who was obviously worrying about the impact of flashing Stanley blades on his bontempi organ sales. At first he tried to convince us that we could outrun our pursuers as we were wearing 'pumps' (Sambas if I remember right). Fortunately we persuaded him that this wasn't a good idea and he agreed to let us out the back, but warned us that this would only give us a couple of minutes start on Bolton's lads who were also wearing 'pumps'.

We shot out the backdoor and over a fence onto the railway line, the sound of Peter Kay's brother and his mates not far behind. Running up the line, we were aware of a train pulling alongside and familiar voices shouting our names. We looked round to see the Leeds football special with loads of our mates from school hanging out of the windows laughing at our plight. We reached the station and joined the escort to the ground, our mates pondering how we'd been sussed as we weren't wearing 'colours'. That, as we've all found over the years, is one of life's great mysteries.

Carve Our Name With Pride

Years before Princess Diana was afflicted by a similar problem, there were three of us in my relationship with my father: me, dad and Billy Bremner.

My dad takes me to games when I'm maybe seven years old. I love my dad and I love Billy Bremner, he's the on field representation of my dad. Just like dad's in charge at home, earning the money, looking after us all, then on the pitch Billy is the top man, the captain. I know he'd be just like my dad if I met him and that those two would get on great. Billy would look after you if you'd fallen off your bike and hurt yourself or he'd give you fivepence for sweets on a Friday; I know he would. When Leeds are on the telly I watch the games with dad and I love all the players, Hunter, Sniffer, Eddie Gray, Mick Jones, the lot of them; but there's only one Billy Bremner.

Billy's not just my on-the-pitch dad, he's Leeds United. Just like I see him as part of my family, then I see him as the dad to the family Don Revie has spawned out on the pitch. That entire team's a band of brothers; never giving in, always fighting for each other and for us. Billy's a contradiction - he's a small giant of a man. Fiery and fierce with the ability to do everything: tackle, pass, score, the lot. There's nothing Billy can't do for Leeds United and the white shirt. He'll live forever.

Except he doesn't. He only makes it to 54 years old and when he goes my childhood is finally consigned to the past. If you never saw him play you can go see the statue and dream - I have my memories of him in the flesh when there were the three of us: Billy, my dad and me.

FANTHOLOGY

***

Don't take this the wrong way but I used to live in Manchester. Before you go flying off the handle let me explain. I hadn't sold my soul and converted to the Dark Side; I'd grown up to be a scruffy student in exile from South Leeds. You might think that you could never bring yourself to live so close to the citadel of all that is unholy, but I have eased my conscience down the years by thinking of it in other terms. Picture me, if you will, as working behind enemy lines; seemingly going about my day to day business as if I thought Alex Ferguson was an acceptable member of the human race but deep down harbouring thoughts of *la resistance d'Elland Rue*.

Or, if that doesn't grab you, think of me as a missionary spreading the word to places where the White light of truth has yet to illuminate pagan reds as to the error of their ways. If you're of a historical bent, you could view me as Napoleon on Elba. You could even look at me as Sirius Black in Azkaban if that takes your fancy. Anyway, whatever way you look at me, I was a Leeds United White living less than two miles from Old Trafford.

Things could have been much worse than they were however. Through a bit of luck and a large amount of judgement we had set up a Leeds United enclave right in the heart of enemy territory. Our flat was populated by two citizens of Beeston, one from Miggy (me) and a Hunslet lad. Rather like the huddled masses arriving in New York at the turn of the last century, we liked to be amongst 'family' so we could practice our own customs (supporting Leeds), speak our own language (mainly bad) and enjoy our own traditional fare (chips and lager), free from

158

persecution. Just to add an exotic spice or two to the mix we had Johnny from St Helens, an Evertonian, and Mad Tony from Swindon, a Town fan, living there as well. They were sort of honorary Leeds fans, in as much as they hated Man U as well, and were thus alright in our book.

This story takes place in 1987, long before the Premiership existed. It was when my hero Billy Bremner was Leeds manager and it was cool to be a Leeds fan. Some things don't change.

We're waiting for the lads to arrive in Manchester. Everyone's staying over at our gaffe before tomorrow's high noon showdown with Wigan in the FA Cup Quarter Final. Our place is a handy stopover for people going to the match and it also means we can paint the town White tonight.

We've ventured deep into hostile territory. We're doing all the pubs on Oldham Street. Fourteen Leeds fans in the centre of Manchester. Imagine fourteen Man United fans going round the pubs near Leeds Market and you get the picture. We walk in the City Arms, or the City Road Inn or something, and most of us sit down while a couple of lads go to the bar to get the beers in. We've all had a few already, so at first we don't notice who's in the pub. There's a few down-at-heel looking older customers but then I see that at the other end of the bar there's a group of over thirty lads our age. As my drink gets brought over I see that they've clocked us.

'There's a few of them.' I nod in their direction. A couple of our group make too much show of looking at them.

'Let's make this a quick one,' says Hunslet lad, realising that we're outnumbered three-to-one.

One of them's walking over.

'Alright lads,' he says.
'Alright mate.'
'Where are you lot from?'
'Leeds.' Chris isn't much of a one for hiding his light under a bushel. The bloke sits down next to Chris.
'Are you Leeds fans?'
I don't like where this is going. I'm keeping an eye on his mates at the far end. They're looking over.
'Yeah, we're off to the match tomorrow,' says informative Chris.
'We're City fans,' says the lad and at once I feel an easing of tension round the table.
'You hate Man U more than we do,' says Andy.
'Too right.'

We're brothers-in-arms. United in hatred. This bizarre version of cross-Pennine peace almost brings a lump to my throat.

Chris and the bloke get chatting and the rest of us relax and start talking about tomorrow's game. Still, I'm keeping an eye on the lads at the end of the bar and on Chris. He used to box for Yorkshire, always training and shadow boxing with his Lonsdale hood up. He's not one to shy away from anyone having a go at his beloved Whites. I can see that the lad he's talking to has had a skinful; he looks like he's been on an all day session. So do all his mates. He's overly friendly and overly animated. Chris is cautious and reserved. It looks like a strange conversation. No one is paying it any attention except me and then I catch Phil's eye and realise he's keeping tabs on it as well. I know what he's waiting for. I'm waiting for it too.

'You lads are alright,' says City fan and he slaps Chris on the back. Chris remains in neutral gear and says nothing. I'm not in neutral though: I'm working through the gears because I know what's coming. In the second that slap connects, my mind has worked out what will very soon be needed: inspiration, courage and leadership, the attributes that made Billy Bremner great.

'I say you're alright,' he says, and slaps Chris on the back again. Harder.

And there it is, what me and Phil have been waiting for. Chris puts the hood of his coat up and we know that this can mean only one thing...

It's a dead heat between me and Phil as we both jump to our feet with the urgency of Billy piling in for a tackle and say, 'Right, we're off, sup up.' We each grab one of Chris's arms and hoist him off his chair. Between us we've got him up in the air like the FA Cup in '72. Except our prize isn't the most famous domestic trophy in the history of world football. It's salvation as we jointly restrain a rather wiry, handy-as-you-could wish-for Yorkshireman who's about to batter an oblivious Manc and get all his own mates battered in retaliation. Everyone's wised up now. Eleven other Leeds fans jump to their feet as one and we're moving to the door. 'See you later mate,' says Phil to the drunk City fan who doesn't really seem to understand how a table of fourteen people have just disappeared in about one second.

We get outside and move quick down the street. We're not running but we're not slacking. When you're behind enemy lines and badly outnumbered you don't pick the wrong fight. Then fifty yards down the road we reveal why we would have never cut it as covert operatives. 'We are Leeds, we are Leeds, we are Leeds,' a full-throated chant by all of us. In the centre of Manchester. No one does a thing. We are proud to be Leeds; we have pride, in boatloads.

Next day, Wigan 0 Leeds 2. Semi-final here we come.

Dom Grace

Leeds Player Names / Film Star etc Names

Slightly Obscure or A Bit Dodgy

Scott / Peter	SELLARS
Nigel / Steve	MARTYN
Brian / James	DEANE
John / Ray	CHARLES
Danny / Will	HAY
Allan / Warren	CLARKE
Duncan / Julia	McKENZIE
Jeff / Jeff	CHANDLER
Bobby / Peter	DAVISON
Scott / Johnny	CARSON
Steve / Patricia	HODGE
Phil / Nerys	HUGHES
Gary / Doris	SPEED
Terry / Kenneth	CONNOR
Royden / Elijah	WOOD

The Lost Card

On Sunday 26/4/92 Leeds were on the verge of winning the title and I was going to watch them do it. Along with two mates, I arrived at Bramall Lane in good time for the early morning kick off. When leaving the car we ensured we had everything we needed especially our tickets and away cards. We were in high spirits and looking forward to such a vital game. All we needed was three points and Leeds were champions! It was looking good for the lads.

As we approached the stadium, taking in the atmosphere, we joked about the dodgy food you usually get at football grounds whilst walking towards the double decker stand behind the goals which we had been allocated. Kick off time was approaching and you could sense the tension and expectation of the fans.

By this stage, though, I was getting a little hungry so I said beggar it, I'll go back to a burger stand and get something after all. The lads said they'd see me inside the ground, so off I went alone. I got a burger and started walking back. As I went, I took out my wallet out to get my ticket and away card ready. I had my ticket but to my horror there was no away card. I checked everywhere several times but it just was not there. Getting so close to kick off time, the crowd was rapidly building up and it became impossible to go back and search.

I felt monumentally brassed off. I had had the card all season and now with minutes to go in the Championship decider I had lost the useless thing. All sorts of emotions were going through my mind. 'Whose stupid idea is it to have away cards?' 'Why do Leeds fans need cards when other football fans don't?' My gut feeling was to be honest and tell the stewards the truth. Maybe they might be okay and let me in. But the media had been stressing all week that Leeds fans without tickets and away cards would be refused admission.

It certainly looked to be the end of my hopes of watching this game but with time running out I decided to join the turnstile queue. Despite the early time a few fans had been drinking and were singing loudly. My plan of action was to stick with these loud fans as the stewards might focus their attention on them. I decided at no time would I make eye contact with stewards or police. The queue was moving quickly and sure enough the stewards were checking for away cards. Some fans that were a little drunk were fumbling in their pockets searching for them. I got to the turnstile and one of lads was still searching. As the steward asked him questions I sneaked past and through the turnstile. I gave the operator my ticket and the metal clicking sound was music to my ears.

I went through with a great sigh of relief. But as I walked up the steps to the main stand I looked up, I could not believe it. There were more bloomin' stewards. This time I accidentally made eye contact and sure enough one approached me. My heart sank and I feared the worst. In a cold sweat and fearing I'd miss out on such a vital match, I waited. He promptly asked for my ticket and then politely pointed in the direction of my seat. He didn't even mention anything about away cards. I thanked him for his assistance and moved quickly to find my place. Once there, my mates asked me why it had taken me so long to get in. I said just don't ask and left it at that. It was now only moments to kick off and the atmosphere was electric with the Leeds fans in great voice. As they say, the rest is history. Leeds won 3-2 and were crowned Champions after a game I so nearly missed.

Sam Jess

Further LUFC Tales

4) Promotion season '89/90 was my favourite season following Leeds. There was a sense of anticipation that the team was going places, the atmosphere at Elland Road was fantastic, and we had a regular minibus with a sound driver taking us to away games. If we weren't at the pre-selected, stop-off, boozing point en-route or at the destination before eleven it was deemed a minor disaster.

MEMORABLE OCCASIONS, CRUCIAL GAMES

Oxford away was probably the pinnacle of our drink-fuelled excesses that season. Three hours after our arrival, we'd had a good tour of Oxfords pubs and were suitably refreshed. We eventually got to the famous game which Leeds were losing 2-0 at half time. The team pulled it back to 2-2 and that was the cue for one of our lads to invade the pitch -from the second tier of the stand! and administer an impromptu team talk on the pitch to Imre Varadi. It worked - we scored twice more and that was the turning point of the season, as we went on to clinch promotion on another alcohol-soaked day in Bournemouth.

Leeds Player Names / Film Star etc Names

Well Dodgy

Eirik / Chew	BAKKE
Imre / Oli	VARADI
David / David	McNIVEN
Michael / Halle	DUBERRY
Carlton / Brian de	PALMER
Neil / Richard O'	SULLIVAN

Special Mentions

Jack Charlton	HESTON
Alex Sabella	LUGOSI
Peter	LORRE-MER
Rod	WALLACE (& GROMIT)
Laurence Olivier	DACOURT
Clarke Carlisle	LOVETT

RE

FANTHOLOGY

*In 2001 Leeds visited Real Madrid in the Champions'
League. The stuff of dreams...*

One-nil up in the Bernabeu

Coming down the Castellana, the ten-lane artery that cuts through
Madrid - wondering if I'll ever reach the Estadio Santiago
Bernabeu - it comes into view: the world's greatest football
stadium, home of Real Madrid, the world's greatest football club.
This is where - later today - Leeds United play. And I've got a
ticket.

The streets are busy. It's lunchtime and people leave work for
restaurants: groups of ten or twelve, wearing suits, capes and long
winter coats as the temperature reaches fifteen. They are calm and
smiling. The trees are in blossom. And somewhere - although it's
only early March - they are cutting the grass, the smell bringing
summer to the streets. Twenty-five years of supporting Leeds
United have brought me here. To a football fan there's no need to
explain what it means. To a non-football fan, you could compare it
to a trip to Lourdes, The Louvre or Las Vegas.

I shrug my way past a few shifty men touting tickets and
through the sliding doors of a smart shopping centre, where I see
my first group of Leeds fans. It's midday and one is already
drunk. He spots more Leeds fans in a restaurant and runs up an
escalator to shout 'Alright lads'. They wave and he tries to get
them singing:

> *We are Leeds. We are Leeds. We are Leeds.*
> *We are Leeds. We are Leeds. We are Leeds.*

No one joins in. Diners, waiters and glamorous shoppers watch as the man's three friends lead him away, their hands raised in apology.

Outside, at ticket offices, the Spanish queue. Leeds fans line up with them, ignoring the touts. There is a relaxed atmosphere. Leeds and Real fans cluster on the steps of the Bernabeu to have their pictures taken together. The Spanish press have been billing the game as a friendly: both teams have already qualified for the next stage of the Champions' League. The football daily, Marca, welcomes Leeds as the slayers of Barcelona, Madrid's arch rivals. Anyone who dumps Barcelona out of the Champions League is guaranteed a special welcome here.

In the huge car park beneath the stadium's west side the media are gathering, dozens of large vans, men leaning against them, talking. In cafés up side streets you can make out Leeds fans under the trees, easing back in their chairs. It's summer here: in Leeds there is snow on the ground.

Madrid is stunning. There are parks at the roadside, monuments, fountains, art galleries, palaces. And occasionally, between buildings, a glimpse of the mountains to the north-west, the Sierras Gredos and Guadarrama, snow-capped, six thousand feet above sea level. The sun pours down and the temperature signs around the stadium now indicate twenty degrees. This is not Crewe or Rotherham away, this is Madrid. And it suddenly strikes me I am not on holiday: I am here to watch Leeds, one of thousands over here from Yorkshire (and elsewhere), here to watch ninety minutes of football.

The Leeds team arrived without any commotion, a Spanish newspaper reports. They slipped quietly into Madrid, landing at 4pm on the day before the game. No-one received them. No members of the Spanish press were waiting to interview them. Nor even the English. No sooner had they landed than the team made its way to their hotel, near the Plaza de Colon. The players had a light meal, went for a relaxing walk and at 7pm had a training session behind closed doors. Security kept out the press. Leeds United had no problems in arriving, except that they had to pass foot and mouth disinfectant controls at Barajas airport. Even though the European Union hadn't adopted any special measures to prevent the leap of the virus onto the continent, all Spanish airports had taken measures to prevent the spread. All the members of the English team had to pass through disinfectant and the supporters had, likewise, to be disinfected. What is curious about it all is that the Leeds players took to the field of the training ground wearing the same boots they had played and trained with in England.

The Real Madrid club shop is surprisingly small, with only a few lines: player photographs, footballs, shirts bearing the players' names. This is not like the city centre football megastores in Leeds and in cities across the UK, where you can pick up shower curtains, vitamin pills and birth certificate holders branded with your favourite club's logo. Here in Madrid the supporters want the club top and the name of their favourite player - Figo, Raul, Roberto Carlos - on their back. They don't want rubbish designed by football marketing teams out to cash in on the fans' loyalty.

Outside the shop, I stop in front of a plaque engraved with the titles and tournaments Real Madrid have won. It is the size of a double garage door. Twenty-two Spanish leagues, seventeen Spanish cups, two UEFA cups, two intercontinental cups, seven other major trophies and their eight European Cups, including the first five and two in the last three years. Real Madrid have consistently won competitions decade after decade. They have been the best football team since European competition began. Everything about them - their name, their players, their stadium - resonates excellence. As every Leeds fan knows, the great Don Revie - manager of the famous 60s and 70s Leeds side - deferred to them, kitting out his team in Real Madrid white.

I go back to the bar I was in the night before. It's just across the road from the Bernabeu and smaller than my front room. Last night's tables have been removed, as have the chairs, the heavy glass ashtrays, the ornaments. It's quiet, not yet busy enough for me to be able to pretend I am with someone. There are four or five groups of Leeds supporters and three men in Real Madrid tops. I order a beer from the same man who served me yesterday. He smiles. Last night I was given a dish of olives with my first beer, tortilla with my second. Now I just get the beer. I make to move away, but he stops me: today I must pay before I drink, he explains.

I drink the first beer quickly, then order another. I need to take the edge off my nerves. Four men stand by the open window. They ask a passing Leeds fan outside to take their picture and invite the three men in Real Madrid shirts to join them. They exchange friendly gestures, the English making hand signals that Leeds will win two-nil. The Spaniards laugh.

Outside there is a brisk trade in tickets. Clusters of Leeds fans around touts. We have been advised by Leeds United not to travel without tickets. But we all know that's just the club covering themselves. Later the Leeds players will acknowledge their supporters in all parts of the ground, not just those in the official Leeds end; the chairman himself, nodding towards the dozens of Leeds fans scattered in the Madrid main stand, where I will be sitting.

The mood in the bar is excitable. The original drinkers have been joined by people they know. Some have moved outside to stand in the street. There is a queue three-deep at the counter where beer is served in plastic glasses. The first songs break out in the street.

We are Leeds. We are Leeds. We are Leeds.
We are Leeds. We are Leeds. We are Leeds.

Marching on together…

The three security guards employed by the bar look nervous.

Then five men arrive, not wearing Leeds shirts - clearly English and here for the football. But they are different. People move out of their path: they may not know them personally, but they know that there is something about the way they walk and the look in their eyes that makes it worth not getting in their way.

Now that the bar is packed, the barmen look tense. I am in the corner, away from the swell of the queues and the movement around the door. I am trapped. It has been calm until now, but there is a shift in atmosphere. The barmen continue to serve. I suspect they are regretting opening the bar to cash in on the crowds. In Leeds, bars adjacent to the station would have been closed all evening.

More than 800 policemen from various bodies and agencies composed the security for the match between Real Madrid and Leeds United, a Spanish newspaper explains. The match was declared 'de alto riesgo'. High risk. The office of the delegate to the autonomous authority of Madrid and the City Council of Madrid together co-ordinated a security force consisting of 400 members of the Policia Nacional, with intervention units on foot and horse, along with police dogs, a platoon of policemen on motorbikes, a radio patrol unit and a helicopter.

Next to me are three men I hadn't noticed before. No colours. They are eating nuts with their beer and spitting the shells onto the floor. They are not like the rest of us. They are Madrid supporters, standing at the heart of the Leeds crowd, well dressed, calm, the same stony-faced look on their faces as the Leeds fans who arrived before them. I realise the place could explode at any moment. I plan to leap over the bar if anything happens. I practice the movement in my mind. The singing is loud now, the queue for drinks ten deep.

Harry Kewell, Harry-Harry-Harry-Harry Kewell.
Harry-Harry-Harry-Harry Kewell.

I make my way onto the street, pushing past the Real fans and the security guards. I feel better outside - it is not so oppressive - and join in the singing for the first time. A circle has formed, everyone smiling.

We are Leeds. We are Leeds. We are Leeds.
We are Leeds. We are Leeds. We are Leeds.

But after a while I must go back into the bar where the seven barmen work like a machine, no time now to be stressed: two pour, two distribute, three take money. Behind me hundreds of Leeds fans shout and drink. Outside, they examine their change and - laughing - throw five and twenty-five peseta pieces on the floor.

I order two beers. The singing moves inside. We are Leeds fills the bar. In the stadium we will point emphatically at the opposing fans when we sing: We are Leeds (point), We are Leeds (point), We are

Leeds (point). Now we point at the men behind the bar. They look absolutely terrified.

Outside, the Leeds fans have spotted three women watching from offices above. They shout up at them, a serenade reserved for women by football fans. The women smile and look at each other, confused, then move away from the window. I notice the top of a tree moving from side to side on the far side of the crowd.

Most Leeds fans are unsteady, clumsily making their way to the bar through the crowd or staring into space, unable to follow conversations. I feel at ease, one of a thousand Leeds supporters, talking to people, shaking hands. I am chanting with a bunch of lads from Doncaster. We're ready for the game and - win or lose - it doesn't matter. We are Leeds. We are together. We are going to make ourselves heard so that the Spanish know that Leeds United have the best and most passionate supporters in Europe.

And next week, when a friend asks about Madrid and I tell him about the bar and what happened, he'll say he doesn't understand why I do it, why I enjoy being like that, singing, part of a mob of Englishmen in a foreign city. And I'll describe the match and the stadium and how euphoric I felt, but he'll say he's not talking about the match and the stadium, he's talking about the bar and the singing. And I say I didn't join in the songs about St George or Turkey, just We Are Leeds and Harry Kewell, but he says I was there, just being there made me part of it. And - he adds - did I know that St George was actually born in Turkey?

The police watch, forming a discreet semi-circle around the bar area, most of them hidden behind parked cars and souvenir stalls. One or two Leeds fans face them, staring them out, grinning. The police look back, blank-faced.

MEMORABLE OCCASIONS, CRUCIAL GAMES

My brother-in-law, Dom, who lives and works in Madrid, arrives at the bar by the Bernabeu. He is calm. He has brought some tortilla for half time but wants to know if I'd like some now. Suddenly, I feel drunk. I tell him about my day, how excited I am about the match. He is smiling and nodding. Now he's here, there are things I'd not noticed before he'd arrived: crushed plastic glasses and empty cigarette boxes strewn across the floor. The small tree is still visible, 45 degrees from the pavement. It's raining. My hair is soaked. And - after a couple more beers - Dom suggests we move towards the ground, just as everyone else decides to leave as one across the road. The semi-circle of police, each wearing a blue baseball cap, a helmet in one hand, a two-foot long stick in the other, backs off. They are trying to funnel the Leeds supporters in one direction, but the crowd moves on them and suddenly it kicks off, individual Leeds fans running at the police, throwing things, then retreating to the anonymity of the crowd, two or three of them caught on the legs by police batons, falling, then scrambling away, not pursued any further by the police. Everyone is keyed up after hours of drinking. The beer has charged them. All the anticipation of coming to the greatest theatre of football in the world is unleashed. The police - confident - advance in a line towards the Leeds supporters, who gesture and smile. Both parties are clearly enjoying themselves.

Despite strong security measures - another report in another Spanish newspaper - groups of violent supporters of the English team caused incidents during their stay in Madrid. The 'fans' provoked numerous incidents throughout the day after they chose the Puerta del Sol as their meeting place. Some of the disorder was stifled by charges from the Policia Nacional. One Leeds supporter was detained for injuring a woman in the leg at 7pm when a group of Leeds fans began to throw bottles

173

in the air, having consumed alcoholic drinks in various bars. More than fourteen of them were transferred to two Madrid hospitals with injuries, one with a dislocated shoulder. They were in a state of drunkenness. Members of the police intervention squad, who were keeping an eye on the British supporters, observed how one of the bottles hit the woman on the right leg. As a result, they charged and arrested one of them. His name was --, 37 years old and who had been drinking. According to the police he resisted arrest and injured one of their number. The detained man, who gave his permanent address as a hotel on the Costa del Sol, was transferred to the local police station. The injured woman was Maria Christina, 40 years old. At least another two supporters were injured in skirmishes elsewhere.

Other supporters from Leeds were more peaceful, such as the score of Leeds supporters who arrived in coach 27 of the EMT coach company wearing wigs and dressed in women's clothing, provoking a great scandal.

I am unsure how Dom will react to the Leeds fans' behaviour, but he isn't bothered. He thought it wasn't so bad. It happens at any big game in Spain or England, he says. He's used to it. People gather, they get drunk. That's all. He wasn't surprised when the police responded. They know what they're doing. But this isn't a serious police response, he says. He has seen the Spanish police in action.

And then I'm inside the greatest stadium in the world: the Estadio Santiago Bernabeu, home to Real Madrid, reigning champions of Europe. The stands are colossal, reaching up to three, four, five tiers, encircling the pitch. Awesome. I have never seen anything like it. Around me the Madrid supporters, wearing suits, long coats and elegant scarves, could be dressed for the opera. This is the posh stand. To our left - high on the top tier - the Leeds United supporters are singing *Marching on Together*. To our right, a bank of Real fans are jumping up and down, waving Spanish flags and silhouettes of a huge black bull. Leeds supporters are dotted around the posh stand, wearing the yellow away shirts we will be playing in. They are chatting with the locals. One makes his way past me and, realising we are both Leeds fans, we embrace. Strangers. Across the aisle two couples in yellow shirts gesture over at us and smile.

Around the stadium is the familiar paraphernalia of the Champions League: huge banners stretching around every stand, black stars on silver, to mark the importance of this, the ultimate club football tournament. The pre-match build up is like a ceremony: the players enter the stadium, two rows of men led out by the referee and his linesmen. They make their way across the pitch and line up in silence. Twenty boys lift a huge circle of material - more black stars on silver - and shake it. It ripples like water. And the music begins. *'These are the champions...'* in a high pitched operatic voice. We have heard this at home games and seen it on tv. I stand upright. I can feel the hairs up on the back of my neck, an electric thrill running through my body.

But the banners stretching around the ground are not simply to enhance the sense of occasion. They are there to cover the fixed advertisement boards, specially made plastic sheeting, to hide the clubs' regular sponsors. And, replacing them, an unbroken band of hoardings, twice the height of the originals, carrying the brands: Amstel, Adidas, Playstation, Mastercard. At Leeds these hoardings are so big that the first six rows of seats have to be closed off because fans wouldn't be able to see over them, reducing the ground's capacity by 3,500.

FANTHOLOGY

Branding is everywhere: around the stadium, on the backs of our tickets, in the programme, on the tv highlights and on the panel behind the interviewed players and managers, shown throughout Europe and the world.

When the aria stops I have moved fifty rows forward to the front of the stand, Alan Smith and Eirik Bakke twenty feet away, looking straight at me. Emerging from among a bank of thousands of Madrid supporters, I salute and gesture, shout 'Come on! Come on!' repeatedly, waving my arms about. I have lost myself. I feel wonderful.

And Alan Smith winks at me. I would have come all this way just for that.

As the two rows of players pass in front of each other to shake hands, I return to my seat and notice a man in the VIP area, his silver hair illuminated by the lights behind him: Peter Ridsdale, the Leeds United chairman. I salute him, hoping for more personal attention, but he misses me.

The players have taken their positions. I sit down. There is a pause before kick off - the referee looking to the tv producer for the go-ahead - in which my twenty seasons watching Leeds United pass before me. Seven or eight hundred games and this is the biggest. And my mother - now dead - who took me to most of my first fifty games comes to mind. I'd like it if she could see me here. After all the years of rubbish we saw together in the Eighties, now I am watching Leeds challenge the best team in the world in the best stadium in the world.

The match begins.

MEMORABLE OCCASIONS, CRUCIAL GAMES

At Leeds, Real played us off the park, the best team I had ever seen, stroking the ball in short pass triangles as the Leeds players ran around in circles. But here in the Bernabeu, Leeds are having more of the play. It is not so one-sided. After five minutes it's still 0-0, an achievement in itself. In the rafters the Leeds fans sing: We are Leeds and Marching On Together. Still drunk, I sing along, surrounded by home fans. You would not do this in England, not among the home fans. It would not be tolerated. You would be kicked out. But here it's okay. They are going to beat us, anyway. We are not a threat.

Except something is about to happen.

Back on the pitch, Alan Smith is running with the ball. He has beaten the last defender and is closing in on the goal. The keeper comes out and Smith clips it over him. I look across to the linesman. His flag is down. The ball has rolled into the back of the net and the referee is pointing back to the centre spot. I have thrown off my coat and am running down the steps, then I'm back up again to dance with one of the Leeds fans opposite. The noise from the Leeds end pours down into the stadium. We are one-nil up in the Bernabeu. We are beating Real Madrid.

As I sit down, turning to smile at my friend, the Spanish fans around me are standing. Something must have happened on the pitch while I was celebrating. I look around me. Real Madrid have gone up the other end and scored. Raul. A clear handball, I am told. A Spanish man finishes celebrating and leans across the aisle, a finger on his lips. An international sign for You're not singing any more. I shake his hand, diffusing my confused feelings.

Leeds are on the back foot, struggling now that the Madrid fans are behind their team. And, sure enough, Madrid score a second. A wicked bounce from a Figo shot. It's two-one. I don't look at the man with the finger on his lips this time. I watch the Leeds players making their way back to the centre of the pitch. The noise around me reminds me we are away, in the heart of the heart of Spain. There must be 50,000 Real fans bubbling now. This is what they've come for. This is what they expect, my friend told me before the game. I try to join the singing from the rafters, but now it is hard to sing alone, the alcohol-euphoria has vanished. I suppress the urge to shout something about Franco and how Real cheated their way to five European cups.

It's raining. Madrid are rampant, playing short passes into the penalty area, moving around the pitch as if all the players I have ever seen before were invisibly tethered. Their forward goes down in the penalty area. I stand up, shouting 'Get on your feet, you diving…' or something like that, slipping on the wet steps, landing on my arse. I hear laughter. And a Leeds fan calls across at me 'What was that you said?' I sit down, cowed and lean into Dom to watch the pitch, fiercely, thinking: the steps are unsafe, Madrid should be charged, thrown out of the competition for putting fans at risk.

At half time, in every corner of the Bernabeu, Leeds supporters are on their feet, bare-bellied, holding their shirts over their heads and chanting. This lasts fifteen minutes.

> *We are the Champions! Champions of Europe!*
> *We are the Champions! Champions of Europe!*

Tiers and tiers of them. There must be 10,000 here. The Madrid fans look on bemused.

A Leeds fan is talking in slow deliberate English behind me 'It is a big honour for us to come here,' he is explaining to a Spanish couple. 'It is the best stadium in the world. The result doesn't matter. We are just happy to have come here.' A girl is speaking to me: would we like to swap places with her - so we can sit nearer the other Leeds fans?

I talk to the couple next to me. I have recovered from my fall, although they still think it's funny. I ask how they got here. Everyone else I have spoken to has flown, either direct to Madrid, or Barcelona then the train. The girl tells me they drove: Dover, Calais, Paris then to the west of the Pyrenees and down to Madrid. Three of them sharing the driving. 'You couldn't get a flight,' she says. 'And anyway, it was cheaper to drive. Four of us came down. We got here last night.' Before the game they were in the Plaza Mayor, they tell me. 'There were thousands there,' she says. I say I wish I'd been there, that things only started getting interesting at the Bernabeu two or three hours before the game. They'd been at it since 10am. She's telling me about what happened in the main square. 'Peter Ridsdale came down,' she says. 'He came and had his picture taken with all the fans. I was talking to my mum on the mobile and she didn't believe he was there so he took the phone off me and spoke to her.'

The Spanish fans pass a wineskin between them. They raise it above their heads, baring their teeth, and squeeze, sending a jet of wine into their mouths. Then they offer it to me and gesture that I should I drink.

The second half underway, Leeds are moving well. But Madrid look like they're playing in second gear, not exerting themselves.

Then Leeds score again. I can barely believe I am on my feet again. My team scoring again in a place like this. 2-2. Mark

Viduka, unmarked in the area, heads it home. I am more muted with my celebrations, but behind the goal I notice a hundred Leeds fans dancing about, waving flags. There are Leeds fans everywhere. It seems like everyone you assume to be a Real fan is really a Leeds fan keeping quiet. But that idea is punctured quickly when Madrid get their third. Raul again. 3-2. The noise from fifty thousand.

Late in the game, Viduka is put through twice, one of his shots clipping the post. We could have got a third and come away with a draw. But, as the Leeds fan said at half time, the result doesn't matter, we are here. We are proud our team is on this pitch, that is victory enough. The Madrid fans expect to win. We expect to lose. I look around the stadium and smile.

At the final whistle, the Real fans around me shake hands with the Leeds supporters. All the noise is coming from the Leeds end, saluting their team, who, having swapped shirts with the Real players, now wear the white of Madrid. They approach the Leeds fans, craning their necks up a hundred and fifty feet to see flags unfurled, to hear their names called out by ten thousand voices.

The Madrid fans make their way out. The Leeds players having left the pitch, we go to join them. I have one last look around the stadium. It is dizzying to take it all in at once, as if it's too big to be able to perceive with just one pair of eyes.

Outside, fans disperse through the streets. There are no scuffles, no blockages, no rush to the bar or to be the first to the car park. People are walking and talking among the trees. A lovely evening. Around the corner thirty or forty coaches wait to take the Leeds fans back to the airport. Madrid fans make their way between the coaches, some stopping to share a few words with Leeds fans,

MEMORABLE OCCASIONS, CRUCIAL GAMES

some looking up to the great coil of concrete in which five thousand more Leeds fans are descending, We are Leeds echoing across the capital of Spain. There is no hint of trouble. Away from the coaches, more Leeds fans are standing around chatting, gathering in clusters, under the trees, everyone smiling.

The next day Dom takes me to the station to get my train. We say goodbye and I go for a coffee before my train. I find a couple of newspapers left in the café. There are pictures of Leeds fans on the front page: a police van stopped in the street, surrounded by forty Leeds fans, some gesturing to the police inside, others holding pints, smiling. There are hundreds of crushed plastic glasses and cigarette packets on the tarmac. The headline says *Los 'hinchas' del Leeds 'tomaron' el centro de Madrid:* The 'fans' of Leeds 'take' the centre of Madrid. *The drunken 'fans' fill the Sol with their litter and singing.*

Two newspapers - devoted to sport - discuss the game, with charts and analysis that make English newspaper analysis look cursory. As well as the match report, there is analysis of the players' arrival, training, hotel and meal requirements. And the fans' activities are tracked with maps and images, even from their arrival at the airport, where, *Marca* reports: *The Guardia Civil carried out anti foot and mouth sanitary measures on the Leeds supporters.*

I get on my train. Back to Leeds. And the quarter final draw for the European Cup.

Tom Palmer

FANTHOLOGY

Journalist Phil Shaw answers our questions

First Leeds match?
My dad, who taught in the adult education field at Leeds University, wasn't really interested in sport (he follows it more closely now at the age of 86). But me and my four brothers were and we nagged him in to taking us.

My 'debut' was at home to Blackburn in the old blue and gold days - a 2-1 win on 11th April 1959 when Alan Shackleton and someone called Jack Charlton scored the goals. We stood at the front, leaning over the wall of the old Lowfields Road terrace, though God knows what my poor dad made of it.

It could have been different: my big hero remained Jimmy Greaves (then of Chelsea, soon to move to Milan and Spurs) while my best friend at school was mad on rugby league and he and his dad took me to Headingley and Hunslet to try to sway me, but I was hooked.

Most memorable Leeds match?
There are so many - some, like the FA Cup final replay of 1970, the European Cup Final of' '75 and a 5-1 defeat in 1983 at Shrewsbury, for heaven's sake, are all seared into the memory for the wrong reasons.

Beating Manchester United 5-1 in the spring of '72, when I believe Don Revie's side reached their peak (and should have won the Double), has to be the best football I've seen a Leeds team produce. However, the 3-0 defeat of Deportivo La Coruna in 2001 and the title-clinching victory at Sheffield United in '92 were pretty damned pleasurable, too.

MEMORABLE OCCASIONS, CRUCIAL GAMES

Favourite player?
Eddie Gray (just ahead of Mick Jones and Neil Aspin, oh and Gary McAllister).

Saddest moment?
As a reporter, sitting by the beautiful Bosphorus in Istanbul trying to come terms with the killing of Christopher Loftus and Kevin Speight. Peter Ridsdale, for all the many failings that would later bring Leeds down, handled a horrible, depressing situation with dignity.

If we're talking sad as in losing matches, the 3-0 defeat by Aston Villa in the '96 League Cup Final was more miserable than most for me. In all their other cup finals, Leeds gave everything. That day they surrendered. As one who spent his teens in the Potteries after my dad's work took him away from Yorkshire, I've always found any defeat by Stoke City hard to stomach too. None more so than when they came from 2-0 down to end Leeds' 29-match unbeaten run from the start of the season in '73/74. It would have to be Stoke...

Best goal seen?
On video, Eddie Gray's slalom through the Burnley defence in 1970, but in the flesh any one of Billy Bremner's numerous brilliant match-winners in major cup games.

Most skilful player?
No contest: John Giles. I admired Billy Bremner, Tony Currie, Gordon Strachan and Gary McAllister enormously as well.

Best match atmosphere?
Time blurs the memory, but the Deportivo home match was like the passionate, pre all-seater atmosphere at Elland Road.

FANTHOLOGY

Best Leeds XI?
Martyn, Reaney, Woodgate, Hunter, Cooper; Lorimer, Bremner, Giles, E Gray; Charles, Clarke. Substitutes: Harvey, Madeley, Strachan, McAllister, Jones (Mick).

Most sporting player?
Eddie Gray.

Funniest moment?
Leeds were trailing 7-1 at Stoke City in the darkest days of the 1980's and the chant went up from the away end: 'The next goal wins it!' Leeds scored it too, and everyone went wild.

Best part of ground to watch from?
The old Scratching Shed which is now the South Stand. I remember being in there, tumbling up and down the packed terraces, when Leeds had let a 2-0 lead become a 2-2 scoreline with Sheffield Wednesday. A last-minute free-kick was rolled to Norman Hunter, whose shot was so powerful that I recall flinching as it tore towards me like a heat-seeking missile. It seemed to have my name on it, but somehow came to rest in the net.

I stood on the open kop, was there for the first game in its covered incarnation (v Ferencvaros, Fairs' Cup Final, 1968) and have watched almost all my matches since from the West Stand - most from the press seats. Funnily enough, after seeing my first game from Lowfields Road, I can't remember ever going there again.

Thing most missed from the past?
At the time of writing, in the autumn of 2004, I miss most the feeling that anything is possible for Leeds United, which we fans had in the 1960's and rediscovered during the David O'Leary era, when the football was as exciting as any I can remember from a Leeds side.

MEMORABLE OCCASIONS, CRUCIAL GAMES

We lost it once, in the 1980's, and clawed our way back thanks to Howard Wilkinson, Gordon Strachan and even, implausibly, Vinnie Jones. It would be great to think we could do it all over again.

One hope for the future?
Not, as you might expect, that Leeds find a Roman Abramovich-style benefactor - Mr Ridsdale has put me off the idea of 'bought' success forever. My hope is that the club stay at Elland Road, run by people who have its best interests at heart and play well enough to merit the undying allegiance most supporters continue to offer.

Phil Shaw, The Independent

LUFC Tales concluded

5) A couple of years ago I was in Vietnam travelling round on my own. I had a motorbike and was riding up the coast around Vung Tau. It was all small fishing villages, very rural and the locals were looking in astonishment at a big strawberry blond(!) geezer with a sunburnt face careering through their village.

I was miles from anywhere when I passed a few thatched huts, water buffaloes grazing, etc. I couldn't believe it when I saw a kid of about fifteen sat on a wall in a field, looking at me, wearing the white LUFC Admiral shirt from around the '92 Championship era.

I was well pleased so spun the bike round and set off towards him down a bumpy track shouting, 'Leeds United, Leeds United.' As I got closer I realised he was terrified. He started yelling, jumped off the wall and set off across the fields in a terror stricken sprint for safety. It was later explained to me that poorer people in the Vietnam countryside get most of their gear from Western aid/Oxfam etc and that the kid wouldn't have known the difference between a Leeds shirt and a space suit!

Matthew Lightfoot.

Chapter 6

'Outsiders'

It can be hard for a Leeds fan to stay objective. That's if he (or she) even tries.

Luckiest Leeds fan?

PRIVILEGED? Lucky? Honoured? Yes without a doubt, but you wouldn't know it sometimes. Covering the fortunes of Leeds United for the Yorkshire Evening Post is, in truth, a labour of love. It's every schoolboy's dream to play for their favourite club, but if you're not good enough, getting paid for the privilege of watching them in some capacity is a sure-fire second best.

That said, there's been plenty a time when it has not been a privilege. Indeed, there's been occasions when it has been downright awful and that's not been due to the football on display or the tired old financial problems. The thing is that, no matter how hard you try, you are so close to events at the football club you lose that edge of being a fully-paid up member of the supporting ranks. It's something that never goes away completely - any Leeds goal at Old Trafford is always greeted with a clenched fist and a wry smile at the Reds sitting next to the Press Box - but there has to be an element of impartiality about the job.

That's not always easy. Mark Viduka's winner at Blackburn during the relegation season was a joyous moment, while infamous away games against Portsmouth and Bolton were soul destroying. Standing outside the dressing rooms at Bolton hoping to catch a quick word with some of the players who had just been relegated

FANTHOLOGY

was not a pleasant experience, but that comes with the territory and I don't suppose I would have swapped it even for the chance to drown my sorrows immediately after the final whistle!

Having watched Leeds home and away for over twenty years before taking up the post as United writer with the newspaper, it's fair to say that my eyes have been opened and my outlook has changed. Being the local reporter on the club is a far cry from the days when I used to travel to places like Carlisle, Millwall, Wimbledon, Shrewsbury and Cambridge with a group of mates during our last stay in the Second Division.

I first went with my dad to watch an FA Cup tie against Coventry in 1981 and soon broke the family tradition of watching rugby league by becoming an ardent football follower. Within weeks I had pestered a group of older friends to take me to Elland Road and I was hooked. It got to the stage where I couldn't wait to leave school and gain employment just so I could fund my football habit and throughout the late 80's and early 90's I rarely missed a game. They were dark days, but they were great times to be a Leeds fan - the weekend in Bournemouth in May 1990 was a marvellous conclusion to the greatest season I have ever witnessed - and never once did I imagine I would be on the 'other side' as it were. In this position you do find out a lot of the gossip from within, some obviously unprintable, but there are other things that you learn and see which don't always become knowledge to your man in the street yet would affect the mindset of most supporters.

There was the time a former Leeds manager took exception to something written in the YEP - not by myself, may I add - and banned the players from speaking to the newspaper. The manager was determined to embarrass me in public about the whole affair, but the tables were turned when a certain ex-striker defied his boss

188

and went ahead and had a chat anyway because we were his 'local paper'. That manager's reign was a short one and it's fair to say that things have changed since then, and the club is a far more welcoming place nowadays despite the problems of recent seasons.

The positives far outweigh the negatives though, and it really is a labour of love covering the club. I still have to pinch myself at times to appreciate the job I have. It's one thing having such access to the inside of the football club, but it's another altogether to be able to call some of the people who have been involved over the years as friends. I've been lucky enough to speak to many of the great Revie side on a regular basis and, without exception, they are a welcoming group of people only too happy to talk about Leeds United. In the case of many they are still hardened Leeds fans and, having spent many hours with Norman Hunter and Peter Lorimer over the years, there's no doubting their loyalties.

That same spirit applies to almost everyone who has played for Leeds over the years. The likes of Mel Sterland, Terry Connor, Brian Flynn, David Wetherall, Tony Dorigo, Bobby Davison, Ian Baird, John Sheridan, Ian Snodin and many others all share that same affection. Glynn Snodin, on the coaching staff at Charlton Athletic, even takes great pride in the fact his ring tone plays Marching on Together and winds everyone up at The Valley. I've also been lucky enough to make plenty of friends from inside and outside of the club, including players, managers, officials and many supporters who I only knew by sight from years gone by. A pre-season tour to Sweden in 2004 was a great chance to catch up with many of those people who have followed Leeds through thick and thin and it's fair to say we had more than a few beers as we chewed the fat in the land of the midnight sun.

FANTHOLOGY

As a fan I have always tried to write for the fans, although sometimes that has not been easy. The club's financial problems were not pleasant - I wanted to cover football not business - and the strain on the relationship between many supporters and former chairman Peter Ridsdale made finding that balance very difficult at times. But on the whole it is an enjoyable experience - there are a million and one worse ways to earn a living - and one which I appreciate every time I drive into work on a morning.

One day I'm sure I will return to the stands, my loyalty will be as strong as ever and I'll be able to renew the pre-match ritual of a few beers. But, for the time being at least, I'll settle for my current vantage point on the periphery.

Paul Dews
Chief Football Writer
Yorkshire Evening Post

10 Most Famous Autographs Collected At Elland Road

(In alphabetical order)
John Charles
Sean Connery
John Conteh
Johann Cryuff
Barry Davies
Ronnie Hilton
Keith Macklin
Michel Platini
Don Revie
The Wombles

The next contributor is a Fulham fan, so what's he doing here?! It's okay, read on...

<u>Kicking and Screaming</u>

25th January 1995. Football fans will remember the date due to a certain Frenchman, the once-upon-a-time Leeds favourite Eric Cantona, demonstrating his appreciation of Jackie Chan movies to the front row fans at Selhurst Park. In snowbound Leeds, there was kicking and screaming of a different kind as our son Liam joined the biggest team of all, Human Race FC.

I must be honest and say that my son's footballing allegiance didn't immediately spring to my mind as I tearfully held him for the first time. However, the fact is that wherever Liam finds himself in later life, he'll always be a Leeds lad and therefore a Leeds United fan. It's his birthright.

My philosophy is that you support your local team. My father is an Arsenal fan, but he never tried to make them my team, even on the occasional trips to Highbury with him. I was born in Parsons Green in Fulham, and therefore the men in white from Craven Cottage are my team. Liam, Leeds born, now has his own team in white to follow. Like me, Liam has seen the early years of his support dogged by relegation, and to his credit he has remained loyal which is not always easy for a nine year old lad who wants to see HIS team in the Premiership.

What of loyalty? In the last season whilst Liam asked desperately each week, 'Are we going down Dad?' the icon of Leeds, the badge kissing Alan Smith stole across the Pennines, like Cantona before him. Despite his young years, Liam knew this to be an act of disloyalty, and so down came the Smith posters, as did his previously prized possession of a teamsheet signed, 'To Liam, Best Wishes, Alan Smith'. Liam echoed the words of so many others with memorabilia from the departed No. 17, when he asked, 'What shall I do with this now?'

Through his time as a Leeds supporter this will no doubt happen again. He shouldn't be surprised, because he'll remember he was born the day another footballer lacking loyalty kicked up a fuss.

Paul Hatt

You regularly heard him on BBC Radio Leeds and naturally assumed he was a Leeds fan. He isn't, so what's the story?

Joining the Party

I may be the exception in this collection. I grew up in Yorkshire but my allegiance lay away from Elland Road. In fact my early memories of Leeds United and a minority of some fans are actually quite painful. So why am I writing in this book?

I'll hold my hands up, I was a reporter not a supporter of Leeds United but I admit to being a fan of the football played during most of my four years covering the club for BBC Radio Leeds. I became the station's match commentator towards the end of George Graham's reign. I remember my first game on the gantry at Elland Road against Blackburn Rovers with Jimmy Floyd Hasselbaink scoring the winner. If I'm honest now as I look back, I didn't enjoy it.

However, my opinion gradually changed as my life became immersed in everything Leeds United. Hardly surprising when you consider I was covering the day to day stories, speaking to the players, building relations with those behind the scenes, enjoying good rapport with listeners/fans and becoming friends with Norman Hunter and Peter Lorimer.

I think the turning point was probably down to Alan Smith. His debut goal in front of the Kop at Anfield left me screaming and the trend was set as many listeners will testify! I nearly lost my voice when he netted the winner against Lazio in Rome and I did my fair share of shrieking after the success in the San Siro.

So many special memories.... I could go on. No wonder people assume I'm a Leeds fan. I was simply carried away and couldn't stop getting excited during my commentaries on that unforgettable European adventure. I would have to make a multi selection for my favourite games. As well as the 1-0 win over Lazio, Anderlecht away was special as they sealed a place in the quarter finals and then the double header with Deportivo La Coruna sticks in my mind for its sheer drama. As for the Premiership, two visits to Anfield stand out. As well as Smith's debut, there was the league trip there in 2001 when Leeds bossed the first half with such a controlled display and Rio once again found the net!

I was certainly fortunate that the departure of George Graham heralded the start of a wonderful period for the club, which meant Leeds were one of THE teams to watch. Now much more partisan, I was in a privileged position as I watched one of the country's most entertaining teams. Nor was the entertainment purely confined to on the field. How could it be when I travelled with two legends in Norman and Peter? If only I had made notes of all of their tales they used to tell about the real 'glory' years under Don Revie. Travelling in a car to the various Premiership grounds or on a plane somewhere in Europe was never dull with those two around. They were great company and what I'll never forget is they were real gentlemen. They always had time to pose for photos, sign autographs or engage in a little chat whether it be Leeds fans or supporters from rival clubs. It's always nice to see them again whenever I return to cover Leeds games.

Eddie Gray is of the same ilk as Norman and Peter. One thing you see from working in the media is the 'other side' of football personalities who sometimes are ignorant and rude. Never Eddie. He was always polite; willing to talk, share his knowledge of the game and, on the odd occasion, revel in winding me up with his wicked sense of humour.

If only some of the players were like him. Before the training ground became more like an army camp, the media used to gather in the players' car park after training waiting to see if one would stop and talk for an interview. It's the most frustrating aspect of the job when a player blanks you or pretends to be on a mobile just so he doesn't have to offer his thoughts for the fans for just a few precious minutes. Naturally, I had my favourites albeit for different reasons than you. Batty, Smith, Mills, Martyn, Robinson, Woodgate, Viduka, Radebe and Bakke would often be heard on the airwaves. As was Peter Ridsdale. I enjoyed a fine working relationship with the then chairman. David O'Leary didn't have much to do with the local media apart from official press conferences so my daily contact was with Mr Ridsdale. It was during a phone conversation one evening that he gave me the news they'd signed Robbie Keane. I was about to put the phone down when he said, 'You haven't asked me what's going on...' So I asked him and he replied, 'We've just signed Robbie Keane from Inter Milan.' A Radio Leeds exclusive!

'OUTSIDERS'

Think what you like now about Peter Ridsdale but I can tell you he is a genuine Leeds fan. Off the top of his head one day he answered a trivia question I set him…. who did Leeds play in the FA Cup the day James Milner was born? I'll leave you to research the answer. He's admitted to making mistakes but I thought the witch-hunt conducted against him was unfair. There are many people to blame for Leeds United's current predicament. Anyone who says it's solely Peter Ridsdale's fault is naïve.

I left BBC Radio Leeds just before it all turned sour for Leeds United. All of the players I got on well with have left and a lot has changed too behind the scenes, yet I still look out for their results. Leeds United must now look to the future but I'm quite happy to reminisce about the past. Just like a fan.

Ian Dennis, BBC Radio 5 Live.

Chapter 7

Can we face the future?

<u>There was no choice; there is no choice.</u>

'But Bill, the boys might not want to support Leeds. You know what kids are like, they'll follow whichever team their friends support. They see Kenny in a different strip every week and let's face it, you don't see too many Dublin kids in Leeds shirts.'

'Look Noeleen, just get used to it. They're gonna be Leeds fans. They won't want to wear another shirt, and more to the point, they won't be allowed to wear another shirt. End of story, that's just how it is.'

'Well, I think you might be disappointed. They've got minds of their own. It'd just serve you right if they wanted to follow Man U.'

'I hope you're joking? No son of mine is going to follow THEM. Better dead than red.'

'BILL! That's a terrible thing to say. It's a football team we're talking about, not a religion!'

'Noeleen, you just don't get it, do you? If they don't want to be Catholics, they don't want to be Catholics. But footie's a completely different matter. You see, it's simple really. You're born a Leeds fan. You are a Leeds fan. There was no choice for us and there is no choice for them. You'll see.'

CAN WE FACE THE FUTURE?

And she did. I recalled that conversation this summer when I spent a few days over in Dublin, with my brother, Bill and his wife, convalescing after the debilitating illness called relegation. Liam, their six year old, had met me at the airport, easily recognisable in his Leeds away strip. Thank God I'd decided to have his name printed on the back and not Viduka's, his favourite player. I was proud of him, a six year old who was wearing his Leeds shirt with dignity despite the still almost unbelievable truth that Leeds had eventually succumbed to the slow, agonising death that we'd witnessed all season and for most of the previous one.

'Who's your favourite player, Catherine?' Daniel, the youngest, asked as we were kicking the football in the back garden one evening.

I paused. Interesting question. Who's likely to be there at the start of next season? Since the defeat at Bolton, it had seemed to be a case of going...going...gone and typically for Leeds, never to the highest bidder.

'Lucas Radebe,' I replied confidently. Lucas would never desert us. They might have to wheel him out on his Zimmer frame but he'd be there in whatever capacity. Leeds through and through. 'And who's yours DJ?' I asked in curiosity.

'Alan Smith,' he replied without a moment's hesitation. 'He's the best.'

Later that evening, I challenged my brother about Daniel's rather dubious choice of player.

'Cath, he was gutted when Robbie Keane left. How do you think he'd take the news that Smith has gone to Man U? How do you explain that to a five year old?'

'Don't know but you'll have to tell him before he finds out in the playground. They're coping with relegation, they'll cope with Judas' departure. Part of being a Leeds fan, remember "Ups and downs"?'

And then as I glanced at him, my brother, the diehard Leeds fan, now in exile but still Leeds through and through, I realised the awful truth. He hadn't told them what was, even for us, almost too painful to articulate. Leeds had been relegated…

The whole episode, and Bill's passion for the club, made me think about my own dedication to Leeds and back to when he took me to see them play. My first game, my first experience of Elland Road and my first time in the Kop. After months of persuasion, nagging and my endless bouts of sulking, Bill had eventually agreed to take me. He may have been swept along by the Christmas spirit, it could have been a rare moment of weakness or simply the right time for my initiation. Who knows? All I can remember is my first encounter with Kop culture and it scared the life out of me. I didn't understand why we had to be there half an hour before the game to claim our place on the terraces. I understood even less when, after the first Leeds goal, I ended up on the floor several rows below, having been literally carried there by a mass of celebrating bodies going *'effing mental!'* It was scary.

'Please God, don't let Leeds score another goal. I swear I'll never backchat mum again if you keep your side of the deal.'

CAN WE FACE THE FUTURE?

He did but I didn't. Ideas about commitment and remaining faithful to your word, your pledge, the contract made with one greater than yourself were virtues I discovered later on in my relationship with Leeds United and not on that desperately cold Boxing Day fixture against Blackburn in the early eighties.

It may not have been love at first sight but I certainly felt an attraction for this 'bad boy' club, so like the type of lad your parents dread you bringing home. And yet my parents welcomed 'him'. Being brought up in a household where a picture of your Dad holding the FA Cup in 1972 has a prominent position on the mantelpiece, your mother entertains you with memories of Promotion Dances and, at the age of three, your brother is able to recite all the names and numbers of the Leeds squad, it's hardly surprising that you end up at least a little curious about what's on offer.

I was in Manchester of all places, studying for my university finals when Leeds won the Championship. I listened to the radio commentary, partied with my bemused housemates and tried to glimpse some of the celebrations taking place in my home city. But it wasn't the same. Not surprisingly, there was virtually no coverage on the regional news and the national news was no replacement for 'Look North' and the like. It would be different now; I would be different. It would be inconceivable for Leeds to win the Championship or anything for that matter (I'm not proud, even the Milk/Coca-Cola/Fanta/Tetley's Cup would do) and me not be there to witness it. I mean, I could have actually gone to the Champions' League Final, *if only Leeds had reached it*, and that's hard when you're a teacher. I'm sure that, with my boss a footie fan and the rest of my department willing to cover my lessons, I'd have found a way.

FANTHOLOGY

Having returned to Leeds in 1994, I pledged my allegiance and became a season ticket holder, although it was not until Leeds had made their way in Europe via the UEFA Cup campaign of 1999 that I was finally hooked. Wilkinson's last term as manager was frustrating and in some ways reminds me of the current situation where we are reluctant to accept what's on offer because the glorious memories of the relatively recent past are still there, still providing a stark contrast with the present and our reality for the next few years. After Wilkinson, better times followed, then fantastic times followed and, as Leeds fans, we savoured the transformation.

Who can forget the dizzy heights, the memorable times of the Champions' League campaign? Suddenly, everyone wanted a piece of it. Smugly, I announced that I had my ticket for the Milan game, the Barcelona game, the Deportivo la Coruna game and I relished every moment. Sharing those times with my family, including Bill, the exiled one, with my friends and those genuine Leeds fans who couldn't get tickets was unforgettable. We must have spent hours talking about the prospect of going to the San Siro for the Final, ways of obtaining tickets, transport arrangements; there was a real sense that we were involved in something very special and the further we progressed in the tournament, the more convinced we were that we could win it. Not that I didn't have my doubts about how we would fare when the groups were announced in the early stages. 'Danny Mills in the San Siro? Don't make me laugh!' And yet, he proved me wrong, slammed his critics, and went on to perform creditably on the European stage.

It was easy being a Leeds fan then. There was no test of loyalty, commitment or devotion to the cause. Ridsdale, O'Leary and our generous board were our gods and all was rosy. Leeds were

CAN WE FACE THE FUTURE?

becoming everyone's second team, admired for their exciting play, their team spirit and the way in which they'd taken on the giants of European football. Even the media developed an affection for O'Leary's babes, for our babes, and I was glad that I'd been born a Leeds fan, that I'd pledged my oath and was now enjoying the rewards. I expected that it would last forever, mistakenly believed that it would.

One of the most painful times of recent years has to be the sale of Jonathan Woodgate to the Mags. Ok, Rio had jumped ship, Keane sold for a song and others departed, but he was one of our own. He had grown up with us, matured into a silky central defender and we loved him. He was no angel, but he was Leeds and what made it worse was he didn't want to go. I was one of those fans who, in a state of utter disbelief, made my way down to Elland Road the night the news broke, as I do every time there is a crisis at the club. A group of no more than twenty people stood in defiance at the foot of the Billy Bremner statue. We sang, we chanted, we made our views clear to the bemused media who seized the opportunity to highlight the cancer that was slowly gnawing away at our club. Fans passed in their cars, sounding their horns and it felt good; it was a display of solidarity, ultimately futile but for a couple of hours at least, comforting and satisfying. They could sell our players, strip us bare, but never destroy the heart of the club, the fans.

Revisiting some of the worst moments of the last two years is painful but necessary and let's face it, the hard times toughen you up, they make you a real Leeds fan, not a glory hunter but a devotee and when in the foreseeable future Leeds are back where they belong, playing attractive football in front of 40,000 passionate fans, you can proudly say, 'I was there in 2004 when we'd dropped down. I saw the return of Brian Deane, the emergence of McMaster, Kilgallon, Richardson et al. Where were you then?'

And so it is that I have renewed my ticket for the 2004/2005 season and when asked to explain why I willingly handed over my money to men who have stripped my club of its assets, I reply that I am a Leeds fan. There is a group of older women with whom I have formed a bond of friendship through queuing for the toilet after every game. They always urge me to 'keep the faith', and that is what I will do. What I have come to realise is that Leeds United isn't about Smith, Kewell, Viduka or any individual, Leeds United is about us, the fans. It's about my nephews who think they're the best team in the world, it's about my mum who writes letters to the Yorkshire Evening Post because she can't believe what's happening to her club, and it's about me whose banter with both the kids and staff at school revolves around Leeds. WE ARE LEEDS. There was no choice; there is no choice.

Catherine Garrett

Forever Leeds

Four lads, each sixteen years old, told Fanthology about why they followed the club. Ed Corcoran and James Farad are from Leeds, Daniel Johnson and Jonny McLaughlin are Harrogate Whites.

Why do you follow Leeds?

Ed - I live in Leeds, I grew up there. The whole family supports Leeds United.
Farad - The same for me and because of the great tradition the club has.
Dan - All my family support Leeds.

CAN WE FACE THE FUTURE?

Jonny - My dad is from Scotland and followed Hibs but I grew up in Saudi Arabia. Apart from Man U, Leeds was the only team I knew out there. They had more passion than Man U, both players and fans.

How long have you followed Leeds?

Ed - Ever since I can remember.
Farad - Same. Probably from when I was three or four.
Dan - Always.
Jonny - Since I was eight.

What was your first match?

Ed - When we beat Man U 3-1 in 1995. My dad took me.
Farad - Against Aston Villa in the League Cup Final. Not too sure of the embarrassing scoreline but I know we lost.
Dan - Versus Wimbledon in '98 with my dad, uncles and cousins. It was a 2-2 draw but we put up a good fight and I loved the atmosphere.
Jonny - Leeds versus Southampton in 1998 when we won 3-0. I thought it was fantastic especially as I was also a Hibs fan. My club winning was a rare thing.

Best memory?

Ed - When we beat Deportivo 3-0 at home in the Champions' League Quarter Final.
Farad - Reaching the Champions' League Semi Final before being completely robbed.
Dan - My first match will always be my best memory because I knew then I was a real Leeds supporter.
Jonny - I went to an illegal pub in Saudi with my mate to watch

FANTHOLOGY

Leeds on tv. It was pretty special to see a pub full of diehard Leeds fans thousands of miles away from the city and the game itself.

Thoughts for the future?

Ed - I will stay a Leeds fan for the rest of my life and I pray that we get back into the Premiership and eventually win it some day. However I would have liked to have seen Leeds in the days of Jack Charlton and Billy Bremner.
Farad - I will always be a Leeds fan, whatever happens in the near future. I think we should stay in Division One to get the team spirit back to where it was in the days of Bremner and Charlton. I really do hope we get the problems sorted.
Dan - I'll always be a loyal Leeds fan. I've already supported them too long to change. As long as Leeds United exist, I'll be a supporter.
Jonny - Well, being young, I have years of supporting them left and so I am sure they will become a great club again.

A Few Words From Our President

I was very lucky that I was taken by my father to my first Leeds United game on 27th December 1932, six weeks before I was ten: Leeds v Arsenal. I was just old enough to appreciate people I saw like Willis Edwards and Wilf Copping playing for Leeds and Clifford Bastin, David Jack and Alex James for Arsenal. The result was a 0-0 draw but the game took hold of my imagination and I became a regular. I was told Willis Edwards was an ex-England player and a master tactician. He was always in the right place. He never ran if he could trot and never trotted if he could walk. I knew he was great.

CAN WE FACE THE FUTURE?

I was easy material as my prep school was founded by two former England players, including the famous G. O. Smith, a Corinthian and England centre forward around 1900, and all my youth was dominated by football in the winter and cricket in the summer.

My brother and I went regularly to Leeds games in the school holidays in the period before the Second World War and we became keen and then passionate supporters. Wartime interrupted all that but it started again afterwards and I was very lucky to be invited to become President of the club in 1962 only just before the influential and very likeable Harry Reynolds became Chairman and a few weeks before Don Revie became Manager. Don had an uncanny ability as Manager, first of all to get good players, often very young, in to his team and then to get the best out of them. Harry Reynolds told me that one of the first things he was asked to do as the new Chairman was to write a letter of recommendation for Don to go as Player-Manager to Bournemouth. He was starting to do it when he realised that what he ought to be doing was to make Don Player-Manager of Leeds, which he proceeded to do. This was the beginning of a golden period during which we got out of the Second Division and rose up, in spite of dire media predictions, to contest in our first season back in the First Division the FA Cup Final and to be beaten only marginally for the Championship by Manchester United.

Surprising things happened during that period and Leeds got a reputation of being a rough team. I don't think that was true, though we were certainly hard, as have been most teams who have had prolonged success. But many of the individual reputations were less than fairly deserved. Billy Bremner was not only a great footballer but a tremendous competitor and, as he stood short, he needed, as they say, to put himself about. But I remember a game against Chelsea at Stamford Bridge when by chance I found myself sitting next to Alf Ramsey, the England Manager. One particular Chelsea player was fouling Billy with monotonous regularity, and I started to mark down in my programme each time he did it. After six or eight, Billy fouled him back. Whereupon the referee blew his whistle and took Billy's name. Alf turned to me and said 'Were you marking down the fouls on Bremner?' and I told him how many there were before Billy retaliated. 'That's the kind of thing that gets a referee a bad name,' said Ramsey. I think the comment had truth in it.

We saw Don and his wife Elsie fairly regularly and liked them tremendously, but after over a decade of management in Leeds, Don went off to manage England, a move that I suppose was more or less inevitable but which saddened us and certainly suited him less well than regular work with his own squad. He handled his eventual departure from the England job with some tactlessness and the FA, of which I had until recently been President, dealt with him with the maximum of heavy handedness. He argued that the FA's ban meant he was being prevented from working in England and sued the FA for Deprivation of Livelihood. I testified for him at the trial (which he won) and told the Judge that I knew from the Chairman of another football club that he had been approached by the FA to see if his Manager was available for the England job; this, while Don was still in position. Small wonder that he negotiated for his future abroad before telling the FA that he was doing so!

Don was one of the relatively few great leaders I have met in my life, comparable to war time commanders in an ability to inspire their troops. It was a sad day when he came much later to say goodbye to Elland Road and, with Motor Neurone Disease, had to be wheeled out on to the pitch to wave thank you. Years later, in fact quite recently, my wife and I went to a gathering of his old

CAN WE FACE THE FUTURE?

team and found the continued involvement of all the players we spoke to made quite a moving comment on those great times. We commented to Mick Jones about the high pay of contemporary players. 'We'd have played for nothing,' he said. 'You more or less did,' was our reply…

* * *

Life in recent times has been for a period more than exciting for all Leeds supporters. Then, more recently, not far from disaster. I am not going to comment in any detail on this period when we competed pretty successfully in the Champions' League and then on the time when for highly complicated reasons we fell from grace. I am convinced though that the attempt to build up a team which could beat the best in Europe was in its way a natural gamble. All the fans were exhilarated and probably most of them will remember that at Christmas 2001/02 we stood top of the English Premiership and then by the end of the season had sunk to 5th. The trouble was that our efforts to escape from our financial predicament were bedevilled by having bought at the top of the market, signing contracts at high rates to compete with those all over Europe, and selling when the financial climate had reached a quite different, much lower level while contracts remained at the high levels.

All of the Club's supporters cling to the one remaining asset: the incredible and audible loyalty of our fans. I don't know how to measure that but it must be worth its weight in gold.

Lord Harewood
The Right Honourable The Earl of Harewood, KBE, LL.D.

Postscript

These final pieces aptly sum up the Fanthology as a whole. They deal with the themes which have recurred throughout: becoming Leeds fans, loyalty and commitment, being part of something which now spans the world, facing up to disappointments, the excitement of going to and of talking about games, anger at being let down by those with power, of heroes and tradition, hopes for the future. Though we older fans still have miles in us yet, the younger ones will carry the club in decades to come.

Putting this book together during the summer and autumn 2004, a labour of love, we have been deeply impressed by the enthusiasm of our contributors. Some are professional writers, broadcasters and journalists, whilst many are just ordinary fans but they have all shown that they are united in their affection for club. It has been astonishing to see just how passionate so many fans are about Leeds United and how generous they have been in helping to make this collection represent how it feels to be a supporter.

We write at a time when takeover talk fills the air. Again. Newspapers refer to our assets and to selling Elland Road. Moving to a new ground lacks appeal since so much of Leeds United's history revolves around it. Having said that, it would be invaluable for any would-be new owner to read this book. Then they would see where the true heart of the club lies. The fans are the club and carry the traditions, memories and hopes along with them. They are and will remain the real owners.

RE. & GG.

Contributors

Dave Barker, Paul Birch, Ian Bloom, Craig Bradley, Richard Burgon, Ian Dennis, Paul Dews, Adrian Dingle, Gary Edwards, Robert Endeacott, Ray Fell, Catherine Garrett, Val Garrett, Graeme Garvey, Kev Gaught, Dom Grace, Dave Gill, Paul Hatt, James Hardy, Amy Higgott, Tom Holmes, Alwyn Hutchinson, Neil Jeffries, Sam Jess, Ines Hoehbauer, The Lads (Ed Corcoran, James Farad, Dan Johnson, Jonny McLaughlin), James Lee, Matthew Lightfoot, Oystein Bjorndal Lund, Danny Martorana, Neil Metchette, Lynn Murnaghan, Tom Palmer, Chris Payne, Mebdh Peavoy, Scott Pritchett, Louise Rennison, Phil Shaw, David Sheehan, Gary Shepherd, Tom Smith, Piia Suomalainen, Andreas Svenby, Annette Tandrup, Matthew Tharp, Brian Turner, Mark Walsh, Dave Weathers.

A match winning squad if we ever saw one! Here's some brief biographical details on some of the team...

Selected Biographies

Gary Edwards is known by many as being the world's number one football club supporter, following Leeds United all over the world since the late '60's. His book 'Paint It White' recounts many of those journeys and experiences and the 'sequel' should be out later this season (2004/05). He used to be quite good in goal too, apparently.

Robert Endeacott is the author of the Leeds-linked 'One Northern Soul' as well as the forthcoming follow up 'No More Heroes'. Not very good at football but he does try hard and shouts a lot on the pitch. Had a trial at Leeds in the early '80's. Found guilty.

FANTHOLOGY

Neil Jeffries is the very hard working editor of the excellent Leeds Leeds Leeds magazine. He lives in London; someone has to.

Lynn Murnaghan is a long-time, long-distance Leeds loyal.

Tom Smith is from Colchester. Don't even think of mentioning 3-2 scorelines.

Paul Birch has played (not very well) against Le Tissier. Member of Leeds Football Writers' Group.

Val Garrett is a season-ticket holder and stalwart of the North East Corner.

Mark Walsh is a mainstay of the Chiltern Whites.

Gary Shepherd is *the* statistician at LUFC.

James Lee has been to America more than once. Thinks Stewart Copeland of The Police the best drummer ever.

Danny Martorana runs the Hampshire Whites website. A self-confessed Leeds Muppet, he warmly invites all Leeds fans to post on their message board through www.hampshirewhites.com or www.weareleeds.com

Chris Payne, **Tom Holmes** and **Amy Higgott** are hardworking school pupils - we hope.

Ray Fell has so often been the media voice of Leeds fans and is currently the Chairman of Leeds United Supporters' Club and highly respected for all his efforts for the club and the fans. He's from Beeston, South Leeds.

Hodge is as well.

Dave Barker is from Harrogate but is still a good 'un.

Bill Gerrard is Professor of Sport Management and Finance at Leeds University Business School.

Kev Gaught deserves a medal.

Alwyn Hutchinson is good at golf but only average at quizzes.

Brian Turner CBE perhaps most famous for his appearances on 'Ready, Steady, Cook', 'Food and Drink' and 'Master Chef, has a restaurant on Mayfair and was awarded the CBE in 2002.

David Sheehan lives in Maastricht and teaches Classics. Also loves Yorkshire cricket and has tried, unsuccessfully, to teach the Dutch the googly.

Dave Gill is a poet and novelist. He wrote 'The Amateur Yorksherman', a collection of poems and co-wrote the novella 'Humbugs' with Craig Bradley.

Craig Bradley is also a poet and novelist. In addition to 'Humbugs' he has a collection of poetry available called 'Dancin George'.

Richard Burgon - is a Trades' Union lawyer, has been to Cuba and, as such, has a lot of friends who are Cubists.

Louise Rennison is a hugely successful novelist as any teenage girl on either side of the Atlantic will know. 'Angus, Thongs and

FANTHOLOGY

Full-Frontal Snogging' and 'Knocked Out by my Nunga Nungas' are part of the Georgia Nicholson series.

Annette Tandrup, Piia Suomalainen, Medbh Peavoy, Neil Metchette, Ian Bloom, Ines Hoehbauer, Scott Pritchett, Adrian Dingle, Matthew Tharp, Andreas Svenby are excellent representatives of the huge number of overseas Leeds supporters.

Oystein Bjorndal Lund as well as being one of the above, has a website well worth a visit. You can find him via the Leeds United Web Ring. His songs are a particular delight. A fantastic fan.

Swags is in Australia.

Matthew Lightfoot doesn't want anything writing about him but will, this year, mostly be working in marketing.

Graeme Garvey is a member of Leeds Football Writers' Group, contributor to 'Leeds, Leeds, Leeds' and has played (not very well) against Eddie Gray.

Dave Weathers likes curries (Tony especially), is married to Gail and is from South Leeds.

Dom Grace is too (from South Leeds).

Sam Jess works for Carlsberg Tetley and, thus, might be a good contact for sorrow drowning or celebrating, depending on the Leeds result.

Tom Palmer is a writer with one of his credits being the acclaimed 'If You're Proud To Be A Leeds Fan'. His trip to the Bernabeu came as a result of it. He has had many stories and articles

FANTHOLOGY

published over recent years and the effort he puts in to his career would befit that of one of our famous and heroic midfield generals!

Phil Shaw is a sports writer for The Independent and has several book titles to his credit, including 'The Book of Football Quotations' which is ace.

Paul Dews is the chief football writer for the Yorkshire Evening Post and the best Leeds United news reporter for many a moon.

Paul Hatt is a Fulham fan and thus a rank outsider. Lucky for him his son supports the Whites.

Ian Dennis used to commentate on BBC Radio for Leeds matches. We forgive him for not being a Leeds fan as his work on Radio 5 is excellent.

Catherine Garrett teaches English in Harrogate - very well - and, in the North East Corner, is nearly as famous as her mother.

Ed Corcoran, **James Farad**, **Dan Johnson** and **Jonny McLaughlin** are hanging around in sixth form until United recognise their talents and sign them on.

Lord Harewood, The Right Honourable The Earl of Harewood, KBE, LL.D, only happens to be the President of Leeds United too!

The Publisher's Acknowledgements

I sincerely hope you have enjoyed Fanthology, Relish's second title, it's been as Graeme has said, a labour of love (exhilarating at times, emotionally exhausting at others!). It's also been a pleasure dealing with so many helpers and contributors who simply want to see it all do well.

Thank you to everyone who has helped, especially so but in no particular order:

Chris Archer, David Saffer, Russell Pearce, Ian Oldfield, Ros Hynes, Darren Boston, Paul Dews, Andy Searle and co at The Parrs Wood Press, John Wheelhouse, Tom Palmer, Bookfellas, Leeds Leeds Leeds, Steve Horn, Jaimes Horn, Leslie Horn, Jason Thornton, The Humbugs boys, Cross Flatts XI, Ruth Turk, Graham Endeacott. And my Ma, for the encouragement, support and constructive criticism. And cooking. And for doing my ironing when I knacked my shoulder up.

And last but by no means least, Leeds United FC and all the staff past, present and future, as without the best club in the land there would be no fans, no books, no love and no football worth bothering with.

Cheers,

Robert, Relish Books

One Northern Soul by J R Endeacott
(Route, ISBN 1-901927-17-2)

Tales from the early 80's of a Leeds boy growing up without a father, a job or even a half-decent Leeds United to follow. Nevertheless, a boy - and a team - with hope obtainable if looked for in the right place. It isn't…

Pretty stories alongside pretty ugly ones, this is essential reading. And coming soon, the follow up novel **'No More Heroes'**.

'A must read for all die hard Leeds fans.'

'One Northern Soul… a poignant and at times laugh out loud snapshot of the adolescent years of one Stephen Bottomley. CHAMPION.' Big Issue In The North

'… anyone who bought their Stranglers records from the excruciatingly named Scene & Heard, or drank next door in the Precinct (possibly the hardest pub in Leeds) will want to read this book. And those who have not, should.' The Yorkshire Post.

'Great read, good laugh, very poignant.' Damon Timm, USA.

'A must for football fans everywhere.' Icky, Beeston.

'(Still) too much swearing.' J R Endeacott's Mother, Leeds.

No comments on the merits of this book were available from Peter Ridsdale when invited. Or Terry Venables for that matter.

AVAILABLE FROM GOOD BOOKSHOPS or
www.route-online.com or directly from the author

Humbugs by Craig Bradley & David Gill
(Relish Books, ISBN 0-9547844-0-5)

'When you can't play football for toffee, you have to play it for something else'

When life gets a bit empty, you need something to fill the hole. For the lads and lasses of 'Humbuggers FC', Crowther's toffee factory works team, football does the filling.

Humbugs, a story of toffee-making folk not giving a toffee about making toffee. A story of toffee making folk who do give a toffee about playing football, about each other and about taking the mick.

Humbugs, a tasty Pick 'n' Mix of chunters, chuckles, cheaters, cheap jibes, cheap tricks and cheaper challenges.

Humbugs, not just a book about humbugs. Or football. Or footballs that look like humbugs. Humbugs is about the bitter and the sweet in all of us, as well as the sticky grey bit in the middle which sticks to your teeth.

Humbugs, because not everything in life is black and white!

'Relish Books' first title, and a GREAT debut!'

'Hilarious, bloomin' good fun - every one who plays non-league football should read this but it's not just for football fans.'

'I laughed so much my au pair had to help me back on to my commode!'

Available from good bookshops & directly from
www.relishbooks.co.uk

Paint It White - Following Leeds Everywhere
by Gary Edwards
(Mainstream Publishing, ISBN 1-84018-729-8)

'Is it a bird? Is it a plane? No, it's Superfan!'

'Paint It White' is Gary Edwards' own unique and hilarious account of the scrapes, adventures and moments of comedy that a life's passion for Leeds United has brought him.

'Excellent read!!!
Reading Gary`s book, really brought the memories flooding back! I could recall many of his experiences, from the heights of the European trips in the 70`s to the lows of the early 80`s. Let's hope there's enough material for a second helping.'
J A Lyons from Dewsbury, West Yorkshire. UK

'Even more essential reading for Leeds fans!
Gary Edwards nearly chinned me in the Kop in 1979 but regardless, Paint It White is a belting read. If you're a Leeds fan you'll find it hard to put this book down. If you're not, from this book you can at last find genuine explanation as to football fanaticism while enjoying many a chuckle along the way! Gary's a Number 1 fan and this book is a Number 1 read.'
Relish Books review.

Available from good bookshops.

And coming soon, Gary's eagerly awaited
follow up to Paint It White.

More Essential LU Reading

Bobby Collins by David Saffer - ISBN 0752431765

Leeds Experts: The Official Leeds United Quiz Book - ISBN 1903415012

The Life & Times of Mick Jones by David Saffer - ISBN 075242419X

Leeds United Rolls Royce: The Paul Madeley Story by David Saffer - ISBN 0752430718

Sniffer: The Life & Times of Allan Clarke by David Saffer. ISBN 0752421689

All of these great books should be available in good book shops or you can get them directly from the Author - please contact Relish Books for more details (**www.relishbooks.co.uk**)

RELISHING IT!

It's Relish Books' aim to publish original and entertaining works. 'Humbugs' was our first title and this, 'Fanthology', our second. We want to give people who might not have had opportunity before, chance of being published, even if only beginning in a compilation such as Fanthology. It is still getting your name in print, more than many people manage, and it'll be read by people all around the world!

So far, we think we've made, in footie terms, good efforts on goal and with luck we have a promising career in front of us. Relish Books will never be a huge monster of a company like some in certain sectors, those which forget the most important aspects of their business: their customers and colleagues. Relish Books will sink if we don't listen to the VIPs - the readers and the writers - so please do get in touch, we need you.

We want to invest profits in to new writing, simple as that. We have no plans to take over the world, infiltrate football club boards, strip a team's assets or exploit people. There is NOTHING sinister going on other than perhaps having one or two drinks too many at book launches and events! We want to share the adventures with you.

You might think you can do better or have comments you're bursting to tell us about our books. Well, no problem...

Please do let us know your thoughts and ideas, we might take you up on them and of course we might not. But we will certainly listen and reply!

Check out the Relish website www.relishbooks.co.uk for more details. General comment or enquiry email **robert@relishbooks.co.uk** - no unsolicited work though please.

Best wishes and thanks for taking part.

Relish Books